"Wes Linden shows us real person, not like a a civil conversation without sales resistance, creating new customers and team members is easy. Network marketing is a people business. We need to treat people as humans. You will love the kind, endearing way that Wes teaches us to behave when talking to prospects."
Tom "Big Al" Schreiter, Network Marketing Best-Selling Author

"As a tremendous leader within the profession, Wes has mastered a way of thinking in order to be successful in this business."
Andrea Waltz, Author of *Go for No!* and *Million Dollar Year*

"It's been said that winning and losing is many times a matter of holding onto the end of the rope when everyone else is letting go. Wes Linden has produced massive results in network marketing because he held onto the rope regardless of the challenges. Fortunately, in his new book *The Prospecting Game*, Wes shares his hard-earned wisdom with the rest of us. As I read each chapter, I kept wishing this book would have been available when I started my network marketing journey."
Orrin Woodward, *New York Times* Bestselling Author, Inc. Magazine Top 20 Leader and Guinness World Record Holder

"I have known Wes Linden for a few years now and he is someone I can call a friend, a brother and someone

I can TRUST. His humble yet charismatic presence is what makes him a sought-after speaker and now the MC for the generic, worldwide Network Marketing Mastermind Event®. This is why I'm excited for the launch of *The Prospecting Game*."
Eugene Hong, Network Marketing Leader and International Speaker

"If you truly desire to build a network marketing business that is fun, fulfilling, profitable, and adds exceptional value to the lives of countless others, be sure to apply the proven strategies that Wes Linden has so generously provided in this fantastic book. *The Prospecting Game* is a brilliant "how-to" where the reader learns how to turn what is commonly thought of as the most challenging part of the business into something not only doable, but also fun. And, it's taught by a man who has done it himself, and done it the right way. As you build a huge organization, you'll want to make sure that everyone in your team studies this book as well. Fantastic, and bound to become a classic in the profession."
Bob Burg, co-author of *The Go-Giver*, *The Go-Giver Leader* and *Endless Referrals*

"Rather than get demoralized by the hype that suggests you have to be an elite performer, Wes has shown you can build a hugely successful business by putting people first in an authentic way, and *The Prospecting Game* will help you do the same"
Dr Tom Barrett, Author of *Dare to Dream and Work to Win* and International Speaker

"I recommend Wes's book, *79 Network Marketing Tips*, to all my team and especially to new starters. I have no doubt that *The Prospecting Game* will be enormously helpful to anyone who is starting out as well as to the more experienced and established network marketers."
Natalie Heeley, Network Marketing Leader

"I am so excited by *The Prospecting Game.* It will make prospecting easier and more fruitful for anyone who takes action based on what they read here."
Barry "*The Book*" Phillips, Knowledge is King

"*The Prospecting Game* is a complete game changer! It offers a roadmap to long-lasting success that is very structured, practical and duplicable. It's also smart, real and insightful all at once. You will instantly connect with the clear, concise words of wisdom and most importantly you will be able to better help yourself and your team manage expectations, deal with setbacks, overcome challenges and turn rejection into success.

This is your heart-to-heart conversation with **one of the biggest earners in the profession...** someone that not only did it, but is still helping so many others to create a business that can last a lifetime.

This great book is a must-read for new distributors, seasoned network marketing leaders, and corporate staff alike."
Dave O'Connor, Author of *How To Create The Mindset of A Network Marketing Champion*

"My good friend Wes has genuinely placed the relationships enjoyed in this great profession above money, status, and prestige!

Wes has a fantastic, rewarding, stress-free lifestyle, and if you want the same, then you and your teams will massively benefit from reading the *The Prospecting Game*."
Steve Critchley, Network Marketing Leader & International Speaker

"Without people, we would have no business; no customers, no team members. It follows then that finding new people is THE most important thing we can learn and then coach into our teams.

Wes has given us a great tool to put into the hands of our team members to help improve both their, and our, skills in this area. Using his own 18 year experience in the profession - all with the same company - he takes us through the various stages that a new team member faces and gives us real insights into the thinking that prospects experience before providing us with the words to help keep the process flowing and our confidence high.

If you want to improve your performance and help your team do the same, read this book and put what you learn into action. The results will inevitably follow."
Adam May, Network Marketing Leader

"As a practiced player of *"The Prospecting Game"*, Wes shares credible tips and advice based on experience. If you want to win in the game of network marketing, this book will give you a winning edge."
Carol Sinfield, Network Marketing Leader

"Sharing the insights he's gained over years of experience, Wes takes us through a simple, friendly, straight-forward process of turning the 'no' into a relationship-building opportunity. *The Prospecting Game* tells us the words he uses when someone says 'no' which eliminate the feeling of rejection, and keeps them open to looking again further down the line.

Wes' approach is simple and easy to duplicate, and is based on a real understanding of human nature."
Andy Waring, Network Marketing Leader and Author of *Make the Phone Your Friend*

"Patience is a skill. It is easy and natural to want everything to happen right away. But waiting? You need to have a strategy so you don't drive yourself crazy. In *The Prospecting Game*, Wes shares a system to give yourself the enthusiasm to keep going when you don't always get a "yes" right away. This will give you the confidence and the skills to prosper."
Mark Davis, Author of *Public Speaking Magic* and International Speaker

THE
PROSPECTING
GAME

How to follow-up
& sponsor with
confidence

Turning rejection
into **success**
in **network marketing**

WES LINDEN

USA EDITION

First published in the United Kingdom in 2016
United States edition 2016

A CIP catalogue record for this book is available from the British Library
Print Book: ISBN 978-1-910138-04-5

Published by Noah's House Publishing www.noahshousepublishing.com
All enquiries to enquiries@noahshousepublishing.com

Editorial advice: Linda Dunscombe & Julie Jonak
Proof-read by Michelle Emerson, Graeme Linden and Alex Johnson

Cover design by Dan Debnam
Typeset by Biddles Books, Blackborough End, King's Lynn, Norfolk
Printed and bound in USA by Lightning Source & CreateSpace

Contents

Foreword

**by Randy Gage, New York Times Best Seller &
Network Marketing Legend**

If You Could Improve One Thing...

If you could improve one area in your skillset to grow
your network marketing or direct selling business, it's
a pretty safe bet that prospecting and recruiting would
be at or near the top of the list.

This is the lifeblood of the business, because that
is how you create new customers and develop new
team members.

And Wes Linden is a good guy to teach you...

What he's done with this book is put together
everything he has learned in nearly two decades of
doing the business at a high level. He struggled, made
mistakes, learned from them, tested new approaches,
tried new things, and ultimately came up with what
you are now holding in your hands.

Wes will take you on a journey through his early
career when he grappled with rejection, fear and
disappointment. You'll experience some of his 'war
stories' that would have stopped many people, but
instead he chose to persevere. And then he'll take you
on an expedition of knowledge, discovering his entire
recruiting process, from adding to your list to how to

meet people, from ways to develop relationships to personal approaches that work, from scripts you can use to how you can follow-up.

None of this is theory or speculation. This is the real-world stuff Wes has learned building a large team. He'll help you understand why the time isn't always right for everyone, that no is for now, but not forever. You will learn how to construct a long-term strategy to keep your list always growing, so you never run out of great candidates.

Like anything else, recruiting is a skillset; one that can be learned. If you are willing to make the commitment to get better at it, your business can only prosper. *The Prospecting Game* is a great opportunity for you to do just that.

Immerse yourself in it. Practice the techniques he teaches. Hone your skillset as any artist hones their skills and you'll get better every month and every year.

More importantly, you'll be doing the business successfully, which your team will be able to duplicate. And that's what ensures you a business that can last a lifetime. Wes has put together something powerful here. I hope you make the most of it!

- Randy Gage
Author of the *New York Times* bestsellers, *Risky Is the New Safe* and *Mad Genius*

Introduction

Why did I call this book *The Prospecting Game* when we are building a business and not playing a game?

Yes, you need to treat it as a business, but, in my view, to build a business successfully you can learn a lot from the attitude of playing a game that you know you cannot lose, providing you don't stop playing.

Games should be enjoyed – you should relax, and understand that as part of this game, you'll get some people who will say "yes," some who will say "no" and some who will say "not now." Those are the rules of the game. Once you understand how the game works, you can smile while you play, knowing that you will win eventually. If you decide to quit the game each time you experience a disappointment, you'll never win, and you won't enjoy it! So relax, and enjoy playing the game!

Nearly twenty years in network marketing has taught me one thing – we need to help our team members manage their expectations, while arming them with the skills to overcome any obstacles they encounter along the way.

In this time I have built one of the largest and most successful teams in Britain with a leading network marketing business. The team I have the pleasure of working with produces annual sales in excess of $125m. I have also hit the top position in the business and have become one of the biggest earners in the profession, so I am sure you'll feel I am qualified to offer you advice. Along with some great colleagues, I've overseen and pioneered the nationwide training program for my company and learned the value of having a positive, friendly 'everyone is welcome to share and learn' policy with anyone from our profession who wants to succeed, no matter what team, payline or business they are part of.

What I've come to value most is lifestyle, choices, experiences and the people we choose to share our time with is what I value the most. Helping others succeed is a very important way that I can give back to a profession that has ensured that, after dropping out of university at the age of twenty, I have never had a 'proper' job.

Along the way, I've met thousands upon thousands of good people who have encountered many of the hurdles I discuss in the book, but have not had sufficient guidance or a framework for which to overcome them. It is time for that to change.

Within these pages you'll find prospecting and following-up advice mainly geared towards helping you and your team relax and deal confidently with what is going to happen during this journey. I attempt to help you overcome objections, share your story, follow-up with people effectively, and all without alienating and upsetting your friends, family and contacts, when approaching potential customers and distributors.

Keep taking action while reading this book! You'll never actually know everything before you start. It's only experience that will actually get you to where you want to be, and which will help you have a better understanding of the profession we are in.

I wish you well with building your business and hope you'll find this an easy-to-read book which you can pick up and look at time and time again (where different things will make more sense at different stages in your business).

Happy reading! Your friend in the profession,

Wes

P.S. Feel free to visit the website www.WesLinden. com where there are many free, generic blogs, videos and links to my various social media channels.

P.P.S. I do many free videos packed with top tips, advice, Q & A and interviews on my Facebook page - please 'like' the page to see more: www.facebook. com/WesLindenUK

CHAPTER ONE

THAT FAMILIAR PHONE CALL

My cellphone vibrated into life, my ringtone blaring to life. I picked it up and answered.

"Hello…"

"Wes – help me, help me, I need some advice…"

Oh dear, it was another team member and he sounded rather desperate.

"I just spoke to one of my work colleagues and told them all about the products, and they didn't want to become my customer – and yet they really need to. Now I'm not going to get my bonus. Then yesterday I mentioned the business opportunity to my cousin and she said it wasn't for her as she's really busy. I tried to tell her that if she doesn't do something now to change that she'll be busy all her life, but she wasn't interested. What can I do? Help!"

"Yep," I replied when he finally paused for breath. "That sounds about right. It's all part of the process. Let me tell you how to deal with it…"

From Day One in my network marketing business, I've been having this type of conversation. In the early days, I was the flustered and disappointed distributor phoning my sponsor for advice. Then, as I started to build a team, I became the one who my colleagues called with these issues.

Now, many years on, as a leader in my network marketing business, and as a speaker at big events around the world, I am frequently posed this question. People want to build their business, and they want to build it **now**. They can't believe that others are unable to see the value in what they have to offer.

My purpose is to share with you what I have learned – the tips, ideas, realities and mindsets. If I can help you prospect and follow-up with confidence, then I have achieved my goal. If you can master these concepts, and teach your team to do the same, they will carry you to whatever level of income you desire; wherever your vision takes you on your company stairway of success; and whatever lifestyle changes you are looking for.

Not only that, but in doing so you will have helped hundreds, maybe even thousands of other people do the same, either directly or indirectly – and that's a pretty exciting outcome!

CHAPTER TWO

MY EARLY DAYS – THE TRUTH

"All the leaders in network marketing are just lucky!"

If you ask most distributors what they imagine the leaders go through in their early days, they often presume that it's all smooth sailing. It must be – after all, everything just falls into place for the leaders, doesn't it?

Surely it's true that if you're one of the "lucky ones", then you just have to look at someone in the local store or smile at the assistant behind the counter and they join your business either as a distributor (who of course becomes a superstar) or a customer (who uses the products or services every month without fail).

Let me tell you the reality of my early days.

Prior to going to my first opportunity presentation, I was pretty certain I would not be joining. I took my father with me to a local hotel to find out what the business was all about, mainly to prove to ourselves that it wasn't worth doing. As soon as my Dad found out there was a joining fee, things went downhill.

"It's a scam, Wes," my Dad said loudly, before the presentation began. "If you had told me that before we left, I wouldn't have driven you here. It's one of those pyramid schemes."

As it turned out, once we had understood what network marketing had to offer, I signed up. In fact, my previously skeptical father had taken the time to look properly at the business model and then he changed his tune.

"Wes," he said, "you'll be mad **not** to do it."

But the business didn't start well for me.

My mother wouldn't become a customer and neither would my grandfather or my aunty. My cousin didn't want to join because he thought it was too late to make any money from the business (strange because as I write this I have been earning from the business for around 18 years!).

What about my best friend? Surely he would support me? Nope. He went out of his way to find negative press about various network marketing businesses.

However, my Dad started referring some of his friends and business contacts to me. One of them was a florist called Marian. I spent an hour with her and she loved the customer proposition, so she urged me to return the following day. Excited to sign up my first customer, I eagerly returned the next day at our agreed upon time. But she wasn't there. Mobile phones were a rarity in those days and I wasn't able to contact her, so I decided to return a couple of hours later.

I was pretty confident it must have been a mix-up; after all, she was super-keen. So I headed back two hours later, got to the door and could hear the television on. Phew! It's time to see Marian and close the deal and then proudly report to my sponsor that customer number one had signed up.

My confident knock on the door brought no answer, although this time I was fairly certain I saw some movement through the frosted glass window. Then the noise from the television went off and that sinking feeling kick in, as the realization emerged that I was being avoided.

Turning away from the front door, I felt a little bit sick. Brutally disappointed that I had been rejected in this way but making excuses for Marian in my mind.

Maybe I had not really heard any noise and the movement in the glass was my own shadow. I could call her tonight and then visit again tomorrow – surely it was just a mix-up and she wasn't really flaking on me?

Arriving home and my insides were fluctuating between disappointed and upbeat. I called my Dad, who told me that it was probably a mix-up and to ring her again later. I mentioned it to my Mom, who at the time I still lived with, and she had a more realistic handle on the whole thing.

"She's avoiding you, Wes," Mom said, with some sort of confident women's intuition that us guys will never be able to replicate.

I stewed on it for a while until eventually enough was enough. Time to call Marian. Most phones back then didn't have caller display to reveal the phone number, so I knew I would be able to call her without her knowing it was me. If she were at home, then I would finally get to speak to her.

I plucked up the courage, still clinging to the hope that I'd been mistaken and that she would be happy to hear from me. In fact, she would answer the phone and be apologetic about the confusion during the day.

My fingers punched in the numbers - 0 - 1 - 8 - 1 (the London dialing code from back in the day). I paused to whether phoning was the right decision.

I told myself that it was just an error, so I should make that call.

I dialed the next few digits. Then, the doubts crept in again.

Just call!

2 - 7 - 9, I finally completed the number. It seemed to take ages to start ringing even though it was less than a second.

Ring ring – ring ring – ring ring – ring ring – Now I was

feeling a mixture of relief and frustration. Relief - that if she didn't answer, I must have been mistaken about seeing her through the frosted glass. Frustration - because I wouldn't get to speak to her and rearrange our get-together.

Ring ring – ring ring – ring ring – ring ring, and then, just as I was about to hang up, the phone answered. Yes, I was finally going to speak to her, I told myself excitedly.

There was an eerie silence for what seemed to be about ten hours, which actually was probably only a second or so.

"Hi, this is Marian, I can't take your call right now. Please leave your name and number after the tone and I'll get back to you as soon as I can."

Thrusting the phone back onto the receiver as quickly as I could, I was entirely unprepared for the answering machine. At least I couldn't tell myself she was avoiding me as surely nobody would ignore all the calls they receive, just to skip one conversation. After all, there was no malice intended.

However, there was still the uncertainty over what was going to come of this situation. Was Marian genuinely interested or was I simply wasting my time?

> **Do you identify with this type of scenario at all? The rollercoaster of emotions over something that is making you feel queasy and anxious?**

As the evening wore on, I found I was investing an unnecessary amount of thought-time and focus on this one person. It began to feel a bit like make-or-break. I was adopting the stance that if I didn't sign-up Marian then the business couldn't possibly succeed. I had developed the desperate feeling that everyone I spoke to simply *had* to say "yes," and if they didn't then my new business just could not survive. How could it if people didn't see what I saw?

I couldn't let it go, so I decided to call back again a couple of hours later, at around 8.30pm. I dialed the number, confidently this time, although I slowed down around the final three digits - 2 – 7 – 9.

Ring ring – ring ring – ring ring – ring ring - and then the moment I had been waiting for!

"Hello!" said Marian in a bright and cheery manner.

"Oh, hi Marian, it's Wes. I popped over to see you earlier but you weren't in," I said, slightly apprehensively while trying to sound positive and confident

"Oh hi, Wes. Yes, sorry I missed you earlier. I was out all day in the end," she said.

I found her words a bit confusing since I still thought she had been home the second time I knocked. After all, the TV had appeared to be on. But at least she was talking to me now. What do I do? Do I tell her that I thought she had been in, or do I just let it pass? I decided calling her a liar might not be the best way to win her over.

"Oh, okay, well…" I continued.

"Wes," she said, interrupting me. "I have decided not to become a customer. I have been thinking about it and I'm not sure it's right for me."

"But you seemed really keen yesterday and…" I started, before being cut-off again.

"Yes, but I have decided not to on this occasion," Marian said kindly, but bluntly, without any further explanation.

"Oh, but erm, you thought that…" the words nervously came out of my inexperienced mouth.

"Wes, it's not personal. It's just not for me. You're a good guy but this isn't something I want to pursue," she said in a very matter-of-fact, end-of-conversation manner.

I wasn't sure what to say next. Maybe I should share some statistical data about my products versus what she was using at the time; or criticize her existing choice of product; or come up with a witty put-down. Maybe then she would give in, and agree to become my customer.

I was entirely unsure as to how to continue this dialogue. I was only really expecting people to say "yes." I was totally unprepared to deal with "no."

She wasn't being unkind, but she was being direct with her response. Something had spooked her. What? I had no idea.

Lacking any confidence, I weakly muttered some words: "Okay, erm, thanks. I'm sorry to have bothered you."

I put the phone down and went up to my bedroom to sulk and reflect.

Nobody had prepared me for the idea that people weren't going to beg me to let them use my products or services.

Nobody had prepared me for the idea that some of my family and friends weren't going to be as excited as I was about this opportunity.

And nobody had prepared me for the idea that even the people that don't know me very well, like Marian, were going to rebuff me as well.

The next few encounters were vaguely similar, people showing, or maybe feigning, interest and then disappearing, or saying they needed to speak to their partner and then seemingly vanishing off the face of the Earth! As I got more frustrated I became more desperate for some success; but with desperation came a pushy manner.

Network marketing legend Randy Gage, talks hilariously about his early days in the profession. He says initially his recruiting style was rather distinctive as he would argue with his prospects.

It was the same for me. My lack of confidence meant that my first few weeks' worth of approaches were very repetitive, where I would find myself falling out with people. I would tell them about the products or the business opportunity, they wouldn't see what I could see, and then I would end up pushing them to the point of having a row with me!

Not a very profitable approach...

Randy Gage also speaks about how he soon realized that arguing wasn't going to lead him to success, so he developed an alternative prospecting approach – begging!

Likewise for me, having realized that you just do not win rows with prospects, I reverted to a different approach, one where I essentially lost my dignity. I would talk to them about what my network marketing business had to offer, and they would have an objection or a reason not to become involved. At that point I would end up pleading with them to join me!

Pleading is never pretty, and you never win that way. Believe me, I know. You may get the occasional sympathy vote – almost like a mercy kill – where someone agrees to buy your product/service or sign-up with your opportunity, just to get rid of you. But it is unlikely they will be serious about it.

It makes for difficult duplication too – I mean, how do you teach your team to do anything other than beg, if that is the example that you set for them?

If any of this sounds even vaguely familiar to you, then you're reading the right book!

What I learned soon after was how to deal with rejection and turn it around, so that a **"No"** didn't mean **No-Forever**, it just meant **No-for-Now** or even **Yes-for-Later**.

I am sure many people will be reading this book, waiting for the recruiting lines of what to say and hoping to find the golden words that will transform their business. But I think it's important to address the whole recruitment process from wider point of view.

The truth is that most people will say something other than "yes" when you first speak to them.

However, my experience would show that they don't actually say "no" - they just don't say "yes." They say something other than "yes."

For example, you'll often hear reasons why they can't say "yes" (which can sometimes be excuses, or can sometimes be entirely genuine):

"I need to speak to the wife."

"I've got a really busy week, can you come back to me in two weeks?"

"I'll call you next month when the kids have gone back to school."

"We have just switched products/services."

"Let us move into our new house first."

"It's probably not something we will do right now, but maybe in the future."

More often than not you will not hear an out-and-out "no," but just something that is not "yes." Therefore, you need to be equipped as to how you can ensure that this conversation is just one of the exposures necessary, so that at some stage in the future they become a customer or a team member of yours (more about this in the next chapter).

My mission is to give you the skills to deal with this reality, which, ultimately, will make recruiting easier and apply to both new customers and distributors.

If you can master the concepts and tips in this book and share them with your team from their first day, you'll build a true lifestyle income. Where your time is your own, your relationships flow and everyone feels comfortable with being part of your business, either now or in the future

CHAPTER THREE

THE *APPLE* BOARDROOM CONVERSATION

Steve Jobs, Richard Branson, and Oprah Winfrey. What do they know that we don't?

Well, if I am here to help you and your team overcome the "no," and turn it around so that it works for you, then we need to think logically about the concept of an initial rejection.

Too many network marketers get disappointed because not everybody says "yes" to them when they start.

What are we actually paid for? In the most basic terms, we are paid for access. We are paid to expose the products or services our company offers to the general public, either personally or through the team that we introduce.

Unlike traditional businesses, our network marketing companies do not offer their products or services through everyday channels such as main street stores, shopping malls, television, newspaper and radio advertising; nor do they compete with us via online marketing. Instead, they pay us to market the products through word-of-mouth recommendation.

In effect, **we** are the ad. Let's not look at it as crudely as this, because if you start thinking about your products or services in advertisement terms, you may become too pushy. That is not how I believe network marketing should be exposed to our friends, family, colleagues and warm market referrals. Or even to cold contacts who we meet during our general day-to-day lives.

Let's apply this situation to the other more traditional forms of advertising, which we will have been exposed to while growing up. The first ever paid television ad was on July 1st 1941, on a New York TV station called WNBT (now called WNBC), prior to a baseball game, and was for *Bulova* watches. It took another 12 years for TV advertising to reach Asia when in 1953 there was an advertisement for *Seiko* watches. Two years later, in September 1955, the first TV commercial hit the UK for a toothpaste called *Gibbs SR*.

Whatever the impact of these ads, we can be fairly sure the well-quoted piece of marketing speak about the 'Rule of Seven' might have played a part.

The 'Rule of Seven' tells us that a prospect needs to hear an advertiser's message at least seven times before they'll take action to buy that product or service, or at least trust the brand enough to consider it.

This maxim was developed by the movie industry in the 1930s after studio bosses discovered that a certain amount of advertising and promotion was required to encourage someone to see one of their movies.

You'll find different opinions as to whether it's seven exposures, or three, or five, depending on where you look. In today's cluttered, information-overload society, with more messages than ever before being bombarded at you through so many other media channels, there are experts who suggest it may be even more than seven.

Consider all the advertisers who put big money into television, radio, billboard and newspaper advertising. They understand that the cash, the time and the effort they are investing into their commercials are simply part of a process. That process is one of drip-feeding and continuously exposing the public to their brand. They know they are not going to convert everyone to their product overnight.

Here's my question to you – and it's one you need to help your new team members think about also. Why do we expect to join our network marketing business, tell someone once about our products and opportunity, and then have them begging us to sign them up after just one exposure?

Granted, the power of word-of-mouth advertising from someone they know, like and trust *should* slightly speed up the process. BUT if we don't approach this correctly, it will actually slow it down, or even kill it straightaway!

Picture this: you're a fly on the wall in the boardroom of *Apple* HQ. It is a couple of days after the very first television advert for an *Apple* product.

Let's pretend that the late, great Steve Jobs is in the main chair and he looks at the Finance Director and says:

"So, how were sales yesterday after our first advertisement?"

"Pretty good," the Finance Director replies, looking pleased.

"What does pretty good mean?" Steve asks.

"Well, a slight uplift."

"Slight?" Steve says, "What do you mean, slight?"

"Well, figures were up a little but nothing that will allow us to retire yet!" the Finance Director replies with a nervous laugh.

Steve leans forward and raises his voice. "WHAT? You mean we didn't get the whole world lining up outside our stores overnight for hours to buy our products?"

The Finance Director is flustered and defensive. "Errrmmm, no. Maybe in years to come, but not yet. We saw a little spike, but that's all."

Steve is unimpressed. "And *Microsoft*? Did we put them out of business?"

"Well, no," the Finance Director says. "No, we had some extra sales that's all, but not the whole world."

Steve pushes his chair back and stands up. "Right then. That's it, I quit!"

Do any of us actually believe that this conversation took place at *Apple*? Or at *Starbucks, Walmart, Virgin Atlantic* or any other advertiser the day after their first television commercials?

Unlikely!

In 1885, Thomas Smith published a guide called *Successful Advertising.* The principle he used is still being shared today.

While we aren't technically advertising in conventional terms with our network marketing business, it is definitely appropriate for us to consider the behaviors of those we are sharing our products/services and business opportunity with:

- The first time people look at any given ad, they don't even see it.

- The second time, they don't notice it.

- The third time, they are aware that it is there.

- The fourth time, they have a fleeting sense that they've seen it somewhere before.

- The fifth time, they actually read the ad.

- The sixth time they thumb their nose at it.

- The seventh time, they start to get a little irritated with it.

- The eighth time, they start to think, "Here's that annoying ad again."

- The ninth time, they start to wonder if they're missing out on something.

- The tenth time, they ask their friends and neighbors if they've tried it.

- The eleventh time, they wonder how the company is paying for all these ads.

- The twelfth time, they start to think that it must be a good product.

- The thirteenth time, they start to feel the product has value.

- The fourteenth time, they start to remember wanting a product exactly like this for a long time.

- The fifteenth time, they start to yearn for it because they can't afford to buy it.

- The sixteenth time, they accept the fact that they will buy it sometime in the future.

- The seventeenth time, they make a note to buy the product.

- The eighteenth time, they curse their poverty for not allowing them to buy this terrific product.

- The nineteenth time, they count their money very carefully.

- The twentieth time prospects see the ad, they buy what is offered.

Clearly this was written with traditional cold market advertising in mind, and many of the people you speak to will know, like and trust you. But, we should understand that often the people we speak to will need more than one exposure.

So let's consider this – however great we believe our products and our opportunity to be, however much we think our prospects will **need** what we have to offer (and in many cases they will), that does not mean we should expect to break the 'Rule of Seven' (or three, or five, or nine) with all of them. If the big brand names we see on our screens don't expect this, then it follows that we should be patient with the process.

In your network marketing business, some people will join at the first or second exposure; others may take nine or ten conversations over a much longer period of time. Let's take a breath and be happy with the fact that the "no" was simply part of the process and take a look at some ideas as to how to work this to our advantage.

CHAPTER FOUR

IT'S ALL ABOUT TIMING

1974 was a really big year in the United Kingdom.

Why? Surely it's obvious!

Yes – it was the year *McDonald's* opened its first ever store outside of the United States, in my hometown of London. This was really big news.

During the following four years, *McDonald's* posted losses every single quarter, sixteen consecutive quarters in total, which is the longest period they have ever made losses as a business.

You see *McDonald's* had a problem. As you may well know, us Brits are a bit of a strange breed. We have manners and etiquette; we say please and thank you, and we a lot of tea! So, you wouldn't see the Queen eating food with "one's fingers," or Mary Poppins having dinner without using a knife and fork. There was no way the British were simply going to pick up burgers and start eating them.

So what did *McDonald's* do to counter this? They spent time gently exposing their brand, raising awareness about what they sold and building up trust with the British public. In fact, in that restaurant in London, they actually employed twice as many staff as usual. Half of them served behind the counters or worked in the kitchen; and the other half were paid to sit in the restaurant, near the windows, wearing normal civilian clothes, and to eat the food with their hands while looking like they were enjoying themselves!

Eventually, something that was treated with suspicion and seemed a bit weird, became trusted and normal. Everyone was doing it, and we all understand the sheep principle...

As Tom "Big Al" Schreiter says, "We know that most people like to do what most people are doing."

Hence the popular term – sheeple!

Now, what has this got to do with our network marketing business?

Have you ever had a new distributor join who is really excited about the opportunity, and then 72 hours later they have stopped answering their phone to you? They disappear into a witness protection program and you never get to speak to them again!

We've all been there, haven't we? In fact some of us may be going through that right now. Our main task is not necessarily to sell on first sight, but we must help our new distributors to realize that their role is simply to give their prospect an exposure to what we are doing and to plant the seed. Then over time they will trust our brand enough, and see a reason to get involved.

The *McDonald's* lesson is a big one for all of us serious about building trust, and a long-term income from our network marketing business. Indeed, it's an example worth sharing with your new team members if they are struggling to understand why they are not having overnight success.

Having worked my way through my argumentative phase, followed by the pleading phase, I realized it felt much more comfortable to allow prospects to leave the process as friends rather than enemies.

There was another key factor in this as well – timing.

Just because the timing is right for you to be involved with your business and using the products or services, it doesn't mean the time is right for your prospect.

Depending on what type of network marketing business you are involved with, one or more of these examples should apply:

*Adie just discovered that his favorite football player has endorsed a protein shake he already uses. He wants to keep using this shake for now.

*Penny's sister gave her some new beauty products for her birthday, so she wants to use these up first.

*Charles & Elizabeth have recently switched their internet provider and want to see for themselves how their new company treats them. You decide it's best not to pressurize them into switching again so quickly.

*Michael & Julie really happy with the health supplements they are taking and they feel ten years younger for using them. It makes sense that they don't want to instantly change just because you told them about your supplements.

*Stefan owes money to his electricity supplier, but is too embarrassed to tell you, so that's why he doesn't want to switch right now.

*Kia was recently promoted at work. She's really been enjoying her new role and increased salary. Right now isn't the best time to criticize her conventional employment and the 'system'.

(Example: **J**ust **O**ver **B**roke - when referring to a job, it might be amusing when we are in our network marketing circles. But it is true to say that we alienate our prospects who are currently living in that system, and indeed most of our team who are still working a job alongside their home-based business.)

*Many people have self-esteem issues that you haven't been aware of, or considered. I know several people who struggle to believe they can ever achieve anything. They find it easier to be guaranteed a paycheck while being told what to do in their nine-to-five job. Expecting them to be instantaneously ready to build an empire with you the first time they hear about it may not be realistic.

It has been said that during every four-year period, the average person will experience at least one major life issue. It could be marriage, divorce, moving home, redundancy, unemployment, new baby, or the sad loss of someone close to them. They might be dealing with an illness, an accident or be struggling to process something they witnessed.

Think about it. It is probably true for you too if you review your last couple of decades. So it could be safe to assume that by staying in touch with people, keeping them informed while building the friendship and relationship, you are likely to connect with them at some stage in the future. Potentially in a future where they may have a different attitude towards life and their current situation, and their outlook may have changed (later chapters will provide more details on how to make this work for you).

You will also have received and given quality to a friendship over that period (remember: make friends for the sake of making friends), and then you will be able to offer that person the opportunity to look at some alternate ways to move forward depending on what their priorities are.

> **Here's a secret for you! The disappointments are essential. You see, your future team members are going to have some rejection and they'll call you up to talk about it. If you haven't been there and experienced it yourself, you'll never be able to empathise with them.**

If you don't get an immediate "yes" and then make that person feel uncomfortable about the conversation they have with you, the timing will never be right for them to join you either as a customer or as a distributor. The rapport will be broken and the energy will have shifted away from you looking to help them, to them feeling that you just wanted to sell to them.

CHAPTER FIVE

YOUR SECRET WEAPON –
THE 'NO-FOR-NOW' LIST

Let's take a serious look at what your business actually is.

Call it what you will: network marketing, multi-level marketing, people franchising, direct sales or social selling. All of them are valid terms.

However, I am a firm believer that our type of business is more relationship marketing. And please note, the word relationship comes before marketing!

If you have spoken to a friend, family member, work colleague, neighbor or old contacts about your products, services or opportunity, and they haven't snapped your hand off right away, then you have a choice. You can either fall out with them, blank them, alienate them, make them feel stupid, leave them feeling uncomfortable, thus guaranteeing they avoid you in the street, or, you can ensure they feel okay about their decision, and happy to keep in contact with you in the future.

When I have delivered presentations on stage, either to distributors in my own business, or as a guest speaker at other network marketing events around the world, I often ask for a show of hands as to who did NOT join their network marketing business the first time they were asked. There are always plenty of hands that shoot up, usually between 30-50% of the audience. That means that somewhere around a third to a half of the distributors that will ever join your team will only do so if they're given more than one exposure to the opportunity. You'll find it will be similar with your customer base also.

So, if you only speak to someone once about whatever you are offering, and then, because they don't take it up straight away, you discard them, you are massively cutting down on your personal and team growth potential.

Up to the time of writing this, I have been a distributor for my network marketing business for 6,574 days. That is around 18 years (all with the same company). Putting aside my initial period of upsetting and alienating people, let me share with you what I learned. I would attribute much of my success in network marketing to my No-for-Now list and how I treat people who don't say "yes" immediately.

When someone says something other than "yes," this is what I say:

"That's okay, because timing is the most important thing. But would it be okay if we keep in touch from time-to-time, so I can find out how you're getting on, and let you know how we're doing?"

It's really good to get to this stage, because it means you got exposure Number One out of the way. Remember, it may take several exposures before they become your customer, or for them to join your business opportunity.

Now let me break it down and explain why it is important to say it like this:

"That's okay…" – it **is** okay for them not to become a customer or distributor straightaway. So rather than make them feel tense or anxious for not joining me immediately, I aim to keep the channel open. For that reason it's important that I make it plain that their decision is okay.

"…because timing is the most important thing…" – I say this because I want them to know I understand and that I am not there to pressure them. What's important is their timing, not mine. As soon as you engage in any clever sales talk, it has stopped being about your prospect, and has become all about you. However, by suggesting that timing matters, you are telling their sub-conscious that there is a good chance they will become your customer or distributor in the future. It plants that seed within them. Don't forget, earlier in the book I explained how somebody's situation can easily change during every four-year period.

"But would it be okay if I keep in touch from time-to-time…" – network marketing legend, Tom "Big

Al" Schreiter, teaches us that asking people "would it be okay if..." always gets a positive response. Try it yourself and see! So, I am using a rejection-free question and politely asking if I can keep in touch "from time-to-time," which means occasionally, rather than them worrying that I will bombard them every twenty-four hours.

"...so I can find out how you're getting on, and let you know how we're doing?" – to me this is a no-pressure, stress-free, kind, gentle and pleasant way to interact with another human being. You're really not asking anything from them, you're not asking for their life savings or blood. Providing you have even the smallest amount of rapport with the prospect, you're not giving them a tough decision to make.

In their mind, they are saying to themselves: *"Am I okay with this person keeping in touch with me or not? Well, they're a nice person and they've asked pleasantly, and they're not asking too much from me, so why would I say no to that?"*

I have always found that, providing they are a pleasant person, they'll give you a positive response to this. I haven't actually had anyone say "no" to this question in over seventeen years of asking. However, I always teach this with the caveat that if they did say "no," then they're almost certainly not the type of person that you want to be interacting or working with anyway.

The reply you obviously want and should expect to receive is: **"Yes that's fine!"**

Once I have their agreement to keep in touch, I finish the conversation warmly and end the call.

As soon as my phone goes away, out comes my **No-for-Now Book** and I write their details down. I believe that every single one of you should have your own version of this book. Let me tell you, technology has moved on from the Dark Ages since I started this process, but I always use an A5 notebook.

As you'll see from the picture, I would simply write NO-FOR-NOW on the cover and the date I started the book. When it is full I add the current date on the front.

I should also say that there are undoubtedly some great Apps, planners, or online systems that can help you track this if you're more tech savvy than me. Seeing my paper-based system should give you the confidence to know that if you have no technological skills, you can still easily manage this.

The important thing is that you have now put the contact into your pipeline. You often hear leaders talk about a pipeline, and this is just a simple term used to represent how, just like a pipe, they have gone in one end and, at some stage, they may well come out the other! How long that process takes to pass through (of course not everyone does get through to the other end of the pipeline) is down to circumstances, their timing and also down to how you embrace what I have outlined above.

I was not overly sophisticated with the information I entered into the book. These are the basics - you can adapt them to suit yourself:

Name:
Phone number:
Email:
Date of first contact:
Any relevant notes:
Date to follow-up:

Be sure to put a reminder in your diary too in order to ensure the follow-up happens, and so you can tie the two together. I have scrolled through some random pages from my notebooks and included below, word-for-word, what I wrote at the time, to share with you some examples. I have, however, changed the names for the sake of anonymity:

"NOTES: Spoke to Sean in gym changing room – he was open to extra income. He likes baseball and goes to watch his mate who plays at pro level and Sean is getting into snowboarding now. He loves skiing, tries to go once or twice a year. Gave him DVD and arranged to speak. He liked the concept but is concentrating on his dissertation for university and finishing degree. He would want an extra $1000/month to fund more ski trips and cover his bills. Happy to keep in touch. In diary for 8 months to reconnect, after he completes his degree – will see in gym anyway to get to know better."

"NOTES: Called Geoff & Louise after referral from Alan. They've recently changed products so not interested right now. Had nice chat about their local church where she volunteers. She mentioned he likes playing golf. Agreed for me to call later in year. In diary for 6 months to reconnect."

"NOTES: Met Paul on train. He was reading soccer pages in newspaper and we got into conversation about different teams. He supports his local side and goes to lots of games. He has two daughters (12 and 15) but doesn't live with them. Is an engineer – I mentioned how I work with some engineers. He asked how comes. I explained that I show people how to build a second income in their spare time from home, and we had people of all backgrounds including

several engineers. He was interested in hearing more. Arranged to meet for coffee later that week. He watched online video, and then we spoke on phone – he wasn't sure if he could see himself working more hours than he does – he agreed that something had to change though. He canceled coffee, and said summer was busy time for him – I suggested I called him after summer and he was happy with that. Made diary note to call in September."

I would sometimes use a highlighter pen or *Post-It* notes to make certain points stand out. It made it easier for me to quickly identify important notes when I flicked through again in the future.

Next, I would make a note in my paper diary for when I should contact that person again. Once the calendars on smartphones became more sophisticated, I used the alert feature to ensure I was reminded when I was due to get back in touch with a prospect

Technology has clearly moved on a lot since I started this process. I share with you the basic thoughts and principles behind it. If you can apply that to either the same paper-and-pen system that I used, or you have a nifty bit of software that you use on your phone or tablet, then that's just as good.

What if the prospect stops answering your calls or you just can't reconnect with them for whatever reason?

Sometimes it's because life gets in the way for either party, or because you have lots of other people to contact and sometimes people just slip down the priority list; and yes, on occasion it's because they disappear into the witness protection program, where they can't be reached via their cellphone, email address, front door, smoke signals or even carrier pigeon...

My suggestion would be that you still put them in your No-for-Now book.

All of them.

Yep, even that one!

Leaving people out because you have made a decision about their reason for not getting back to you will prove to be costly. Even if you are right about leaving someone out of your No-for-Now list nine times out of ten, the one time you're wrong about, will still be expensive for you.

That person might have ended up being a recurring customer for you, or a distributor who builds a big team.

If you edit your list, you'll edit your income.

Here's an example in one of my No-for-Now books of where I started the process but was unable to pin down a get-together:

'NOTES: Reconnected with Pip & Karoline on Facebook. They are settled in area now and kids seem happy in new school. Enjoying having more space, bigger garden etc. Recently bought hot tub! Chatted on private message with Pip. Didn't tell him much at all, except it would be good to get together and show them more about what I do, as there would definitely be benefits in it for them. Didn't manage to pin down time – they went on holiday and then I tried to connect with him again. He hasn't responded to a couple of messages now, so rather than hound him, I will contact again in 3 months.'

However you choose to use your No-for-Now book, whether paper or technology, if you adopt these principles and teach them to your team, you will build a **far** larger income than you would have done by treating every "no" as the final answer.

CHAPTER SIX

FOLLOWING UP WITH YOUR NO-FOR-NOWS

"Yeah, but what do I say when I want to follow-up?"

It's one thing being diligent enough to put these details into a No-for-Now book and your diary, but what about actually following up with them? How do you do it?

You have two choices as to how you work this: either make it salesman-like and clinical; or make it friendly and relaxed. I always opt for the latter and in my experience prospects respond to that approach much more positively.

I like to have the mindset that I am simply making friends for the sake of making friends; that I am developing a relationship for the sake of developing a relationship. As soon as people feel you are looking at them with dollar signs in your eyes, you have lost them.

So keep it real and keep it human.

When it's time to call someone back, I re-read the notes I originally made, and then I call to catch-up. The conversation will go something like this:

"Hi Mike, it's Wes – How are you and Jayne doing?" – is a simple way to start a conversation when you haven't spoken to someone for a while.

"I remember last time we spoke you mentioned you were booking a holiday to Florida – I would love to go there sometime – How was it?" – Continue the conversation with simple, friendly chit-chat based on what you recall or what your No-for-Now book tells you.

"And is work going well?" – This would be a fairly standard question for me to ask. In part to keep the interaction about *them*, plus, this is the type of question that can give you some clues as to whether there's an appropriate angle for you to discuss your products, services or business opportunity with them.

What is absolutely key to this process is that you do not attempt to interrupt with your own bigger and better story all about you.

Examples to avoid:

"Sorry to hear you've been unwell. Let me tell you about my visit to the hospital recently and the mix-up they made with my test results."

"Shame you only had a week away, I always like to go for a minimum of two weeks."

Avoid the need to try and top their stories; the more you're talking, the less engaged they'll be.

Be interested, not interesting.

Personally, I see how the conversation goes from here and make a judgment call – if they are someone you know, it may run on quite easily, whereas if it was someone who was more of a stranger then you need to read the signs as to how much conversation is welcome.

If appropriate (and only if appropriate) I will then move the conversation around to my network marketing products or business opportunity:

"Lyn, last time we spoke, I showed you how the health shakes/face-cream/eyelashes/coffee/Discount Club/45-day fitness plan/supplements/utility savings/greeting cards that I have been using could benefit you too, and it wasn't the right time for you.

So I was just curious whether now might be a better time for you to take another look?"

If you have had an event, a new promotion or improvements to your product line since the last time you spoke, then you could alter the ending (with enthusiasm!) to something like this:

"…So I was just curious whether now might be a better time for you to take another look, because

we've had some really exciting upgrades to our product that I wanted to show you?"

If there's some interest then I recommend you try and get face-to-face with them as soon as possible. I always like to use the alternative close:

"Well, let's get together, Monday or Tuesday. What's best for you?" and once they respond, you can whittle that down further by asking *"Afternoon or evening? Would six o'clock or eight be better?"*

You tend to minimize the chances of them saying "no" if you offer them an alternative. If they can't do the times you propose then they tend to offer you a suggestion as to when they can do.

Example: "I can't do Monday as we have parents' evening, and Tuesday I am working late, but I am free on Friday."

The approach is very similar if my angle with the person is related to the business opportunity, for example:

"Steve, last time we spoke I showed you how you can build a business in your spare time from home, to help pay the school fees for Angie and Mikey. It wasn't the right time for you then because of the new job. But I was just curious whether now might be a better time for you to take another look at building up that extra income to help with the school fees we discussed?"

Again, if there have been some exciting new products or services, you can include that information also:

"...but I was just curious whether now might be a better time for you to take another look at building up that extra income to help with the school fees we discussed, as we've had a couple of new announcements which are really exciting and I would love to show you?"

What happens if they say something *other* than "yes", as they did the time before?

Can you guess what I'll say?

It's pretty simple – you might have heard it somewhere before…

"That's okay, because timing is the most important thing. But would it be okay if we keep in touch from time-to-time so I can find out how you're getting on, and let you know how we're doing?"

That's right, I say the same thing that I said three months, six months or a year earlier! Because you've been pleasant and taken an interest in them and not pressured them at all, I have always found this response to be naturally positive.

Great news – they've now had exposure Number Two!

So you simply update your No-for-Now notes and add to your diary the date for the next exposure.

You should decide when you feel it is appropriate to reconnect with them, which may be a few weeks or a few months, or longer. Make a judgment depending on your relationship with them and how it was left. I recommend you reapproach them in the exact same manner. Be pleasant, relaxed and conversational – just checking-in again, that's all.

These conversations will often reveal some further details about the person; their state of mind, whether they love or hate their job, their family situation, how much they travel, what frustrations they have. These notes can be added to your No-for-Now book and may well give you a different angle to build your relationship with them, and who knows where that will lead?

So let's say that you get to the end of your next exposure, and it's still not the right time for them to get involved with your business, either as someone who is using the products, or as a distributor. What do you say next?

I bet you've guessed it - I'm sure you can work it out! Just in case you haven't caught on yet, this is what I say:

"That's okay, because timing is the most important thing. But would it be okay if we keep in touch from time-to-time, so I can find out how you're getting on, and let you know how we're doing?"

The wonderful news is, they've now had exposure Number Three!

Some people will argue that an exposure is a full-on presentation, once your prospect has had a product demonstration, watched a video, spoken to your upline, and seen the compensation plan. But I disagree entirely. If this business is about building relationships, then my view is that an exposure is just checking-in with them and having a chat. A simple friendly call will remind them what you do and, significantly, that you are still doing it. You will be surprised by how many of your contacts will think, *"I'll see how they do first"* even if they don't say so. The longer they can see you are still building your business, the more real and viable it becomes for them.

Exposure Three can lead to exposure Four which can lead to exposure Five, and so on. If we are serious about our network marketing business we should be okay with the idea that it may take several exposures, over a period of time, for some people to join our business or become a member of our team.

My experience shows that by continuing this process you build a massive pipeline of people on your No-for-Now list, and over time, some of them will join you.

> **Think about it: Is there a better chance of some of those people becoming your customer or team member if you keep in touch with them from time-to-time, or if you completely discard them as soon as they don't jump on board the first time you speak to them?**

For a keynote speech I did at the Network Marketing Mastermind Event® in 2013, I prepared a video with the help of some pigeons! I attempted to demonstrate the difference between the subtle, calm approach, versus the bombastic, annoying approach. Check it out at: www.weslinden.com/pigeon

LEADER'S STORY:

Natalie Heeley has had a magnificent journey to becoming one of the top distributors in the world in her network marketing business. However, it didn't start this way for the single mom. Her fascinating story will highlight for anyone, the importance of understanding that a 'no' is just a No-for-Now:

"It's not your job to convince people. If they get involved, it will only be when the time is right for them.

I understand the frustration you feel. You know the person in front of you would be absolutely fantastic at your business, but they just keep saying no.

Imagine how my poor Mom felt when I said no to joining her network marketing business. She was already successful and wanted her children to enjoy the same financial freedom. But I said no, my sister said no and my brother said no.

We even banned her from speaking about her business when we were in the room and we would roll our eyes if we heard her talking about the business. It never occurred to any of us back then that we had every reason to be impressed and proud of all that she had achieved.

After ten years of saying no, suddenly the timing was right. My children were young and money was tight. I started to enjoy the extra income that paid for family treats. It wasn't until my son informed his preschool teacher that we were going to *Disneyland* that I finally realized it was a business that I needed to take seriously, and not just a hobby. I couldn't let my son down. So I needed to increase my income to pay for the holiday.

I finally found my reason for doing the business –
I wanted financial freedom for my family.

My children became my why.

It took a further seven and a half years before
the timing was right for my younger sister to join
us and it was nine years before my older brother
joined us. In the same way my Mom didn't pester
me, I didn't pester them. Just the occasional
conversation around how the business was
going and how it might benefit them.

So don't get upset or frustrated when someone
won't join you. Move on. Build your business and
remember - No doesn't always mean Never."

CHAPTER SEVEN

SOCIAL MEDIA – THE CHANCE TO MAKE OR BREAK YOUR BUSINESS

I'm always surprised by the people who turn social media into anti-social media, and then wonder why their friends have stopped speaking to them, and their family doesn't answer their calls anymore.

Whether you have talked to people in your sphere of influence or not, if you are connected with them on *Facebook* they'll be watching you. Consciously or unconsciously, they will be there, in the background, peering over the virtual backyard fence.

If your wall is full of drunken pictures, foul-mouthed rants about your neighbor and their noisy dog, prejudiced and divisive opinions, or moans about your ex-partner, you are unlikely to attract people to you.

If you fast-forward a few days, weeks or months when you want to get in touch with *Facebook* contacts about your new business, you may well find they are unwilling to listen to you.

Your job is to make them want to spend time with you. You need to create a feeling of curiosity about you and your lifestyle.

Once someone has been added to your No-for-Now list, you need to be very aware of what they will see if you are connected with them on *Facebook*.

Are they going to see you as someone who is enjoying a positive life? If your products are health or beauty related, can people see you are passionate about them and appearing to be benefiting from them? Are they going to see you as someone who is living a powerful and determined life? Are you upbeat and empowering, or sniping and cynical? Be honest with yourself - are you giving off an impression that is going to have people wanting to follow you and be led by you?

Don't get me wrong, if you are on the way up and don't yet have material and financial proof of your success thus far, I'm not saying you should invent things. But I am a big believer that we need to leave our baggage at home or work and avoid sharing dramas. Stop whining about neighbors, friends, ex-partners, work colleagues, television celebrities and the government. Instead, share more prosperous insights. Post positive thoughts and uplifting stories about great service you have received or cool things that happen in your day. Use fun pictures of all the events you are going to and the people you are meeting.

You can do an occasional congratulations message to celebrate a colleague you admire on their progress. It doesn't have to be someone in your team – it is the story that matters most. If told in the right way you can share inspiring stories and at the same time plant seeds in the mind of the reader about the fact that other ordinary people, with similar backgrounds to them, are doing this too.

Here are a couple of real-life examples that I have used myself on *Facebook*:

Lynn and Paul

"Big well done to Lynn and Paul who achieved a significant promotion in their part-time, home-based business!

"Both of them are prison officers but after just a couple of years of spare-time effort, they've been able to reduce the number of shifts they do in that obviously difficult environment, and they're continuing to push towards their own financial and personal goals.

Well done also to Alun & Roz, and Sheila & John who have supported and cheered them on, and of course all the folks in their growing team.

Daz and Dee

"I'm really pleased that my good friends, Daz and Dee, have achieved a promotion in their home-based business that they work in their spare time. Daz is a police officer and Dee has a beauty business, as well as being busy parents of four children, all under the age of eleven.

"Although only involved with our business for less than a year, they're already able to have an extra family day or two somewhere fun each month with the extra income they are generating. While they have their eyes set on retiring from their full-time jobs, the difference they've made to their family time is already significant.

"Well done guys! And a cheer too for both Ed and Anna who have been providing great team support."

WARNING! Don't be surprised if a few of the people you are connected with take offense at any additional positivity. For some people the glass is half-empty, not half-full, and they will not enjoy seeing other people having a good time. That's their problem, not yours. Sadly, there are some people who can't be happy for themselves, let alone anyone else.

A couple of years ago, I travelled to a lovely part of Marbella, Spain with Art and Ann Jonak. They are legends in our profession, having built a significant business. They share their knowledge as well, organizing and running the Network Marketing Mastermind Event®, for networkers of any level from all over the world, which has been running for more than a decade. Art and Ann have also educated and empowered hundreds of thousands of people, not just through these events, but also through their free, generic videos. Take a look at www.mastermindevent.com/blog.

They were in Spain, enjoying time with their lovely family, and my partner and I popped over to spend a few days with them, creating great memories. One of the things I learned from Art was that, when he speaks to any prospect, whether it's for his products or his opportunity, he always asks for their contact details before parting. Instead of swapping business cards, he simply hands over his phone and asks, "Would you put in your contact details so we can stay connected?"

He then finds them on *Facebook* and sends them a "friend request." If he can't find them, he simply reaches out and asks, "What is the best way for me to add you on *Facebook*?"

With this simple and friendly technique, he builds new relationships everywhere he goes. Plus, *Facebook* is a great way to get to know peoples' hobbies, families and goals.

While this may not always be possible with every connection we make, it is certainly good practice and well worth adding to your armory.

It is also worth getting to grips with how to build lists on *Facebook*. It means that if you want to share an update about your grandfather's arthritis, you can ensure that only your family can see the post. Or, if you have something relevant to your day job you wish to share, then only your work colleagues get to see it.

***Facebook* lists is a very simple feature to use.**

To create a new list:

1. Scroll down to Friends on the left side of your News Feed. Hover over Friends and click More.

2. Click Create List.

3. Enter a name for your list and the names of friends you'd like to add. Keep in mind you can add or remove friends from your lists at any time.

4. Click Create.

The best way to interact with your No-for-Now prospects on *Facebook* is thoughtfully, rather than tactically. If you focus on building and strengthening relationships, rather than shouting **"BUY MY STUFF!"** all over your wall, you will win in the long term.

For example, you should be sure to "like" and comment on their posts regularly to show interest in what they are up to, and this way you genuinely learn more about them. Inevitably, this also strengthens their positivity towards you. Plus it means your *Facebook* friends actually become your real friends.

Why not send them a personal 'happy birthday' private message? You can do this through *Facebook* or text, via *WhatsApp*, or even by picking the phone up and calling them. It is more personal and thoughtful rather than posting on their wall where it will likely get lost amongst the 400 other birthday messages. Likewise, congratulate them personally when they pass their driving test or get a promotion at work, or their daughter gets into dance school. Challenge yourself to initiate more "just to talk" phone calls, to your friends and family, instead of just texting. Richer conversation flows over the phone and it makes you stand out as someone who genuinely cares; plus, then you don't only call when you are hoping to talk business.

It makes you stand out and shines the light on you, which in turn is extra exposure for them to your business, and it means they are thinking of you again.

It also means that you are learning more about them and their passions, which will help from both a business perspective, and from the angle of friendship. This is another very important reason to keep your profile looking positive and upbeat.

Ultimately my aim is always to continue to make friends for the sake of making friends, and to strengthen friendships for the sake of strengthening friendships. My priority is to engage with them, not to sell to them.

Please avoid at all costs the desire to plaster your *Facebook* with advertisements for your products and business opportunity. The **'BUY MY STUFF'** status updates will simply stop people engaging with your posts, which means they will not get the chance to see your positive messages either.

In my first book, *79 Network Marketing Tips for Fast-Track Success*, I cover this topic and share the following advice with regards to writing status updates. These suggested posts should be varied and interspersed between other life stuff:

"It's great to be working only four days a week now."

"Sports day was fun – Henry and Freddie did well – but why was I the only dad there?"

"Loving the clever, new gizmo which keeps food fresh for longer."

"My energy bill is here! It seems silly to get excited about it I know – but now I do!"

"Looking forward to our little break next weekend – three holidays in a year would have been impossible a couple of years ago."

"Just enjoying a coffee with Kathy and Paul and then off to the gym. Love the spare time my new business gives me."

"What a fantastic evening – I LOVE being around such positive people - so different from my normal workplace."

"Bizarre to think I am 15lbs lighter now, in just four months."

"I see XYZ are putting up their prices again. I'm glad we don't need to worry about that anymore."

"Got told I looked 25 today. Not bad for a 42-year old! Loving my new skincare products."

"Alison starts school tomorrow but I'm so glad I'm one of those moms who can work from home for myself now rather than go back to work."

Creating curiosity with those in your social circle, rather than directly selling to them, is far more likely to encourage people to send you a response or a direct message asking what you are up to. Although this may not happen the first time they see your post, it will have a compound effect and over time people will notice a difference and comment.

Personally, I believe you should ensure at least four out of five of your status updates are free of any obvious

business links. That way people stay more engaged –
remember, **it's social media not anti-social media**.

I recently saw on *Facebook* someone blasting their
friends for not supporting their home-based business.
They observed they had thirty-four likes for their moan
about the local council, fifty-six likes for the story about
a cat, and two likes about their network marketing
products (which had been written as a blatant sales
pitch). If that doesn't tell them (and you) all they
needed to know, then probably nothing will.

I cannot be any more direct than this – if you use social
media badly, your No-for-Now prospects will never
join you, no matter how many exposures they have.
The same applies to those you have not yet spoken
to about your business. In fact, they will become No-
Forevers, so tread carefully.

CHAPTER EIGHT

THE SILLY THINGS WE SAY TO OUR TEAMS – AND HOW WE CAN HELP THEM MORE!

I'm nearly 40 years old!

I know you're shocked!

Yes indeed, at the time of writing this book I am in the latter part of my 30s – and I still get messages from my lovely mother, telling me to dress up warmly!

I know you're shocked! But I really am in my late 30s - which I know will surprise anyone who has seen me, as I clearly only look 23…

Let me give you an example of an email I received recently from my Mom:

Now, I love my Mom and she's done a great job helping me grow up. She gives me lots of good advice. But, like all moms, she also offered me lots of guidance that was well meaning but in some cases unhelpful in the long term.

For example, "*Don't speak to strangers.*" This was very helpful from birth until my mid-teens, but then when I wanted to start dating, it became less than useful! It's definitely not advice that is of any use when you want to start a job, and it really is the worst instruction you can possibly follow when you are hoping to be successful in building your network marketing business.

You will doubtless have been on the receiving end of a fair amount of well-meaning, but not always helpful, advice. Some of it may even have come from the leaders in your business and speakers you see at events on stage. For those of you who have already started building a team, you may well now be passing the advice to your downline.

It is said with the best intentions by people who are genuinely wishing to help, but maybe we could be more helpful with some extra thought.

In the quest for finding people that will say "yes," we know that lots of people won't say "yes" to begin with. This is the source of much bewilderment, frustration and disappointment for distributors, and yet sometimes we are told: "you can't say the wrong thing to the right person – and you can't say the right thing to the wrong person."

Is that true though?

I think not and I'll tell you why.

In 1997, I had just turned twenty and was a student at university living on the breadline. I had been invited to my first opportunity presentation and felt excited to go find out about what would become my first and only network marketing business.

But there were two immediate problems:

Firstly, I didn't drive and had no way of getting to the meeting.

Secondly, I didn't have any money for the joining fee.

So I asked my Dad, who had a successful, conventional publishing business, to come along with me. I said to him, "Dad, I want to be like you and become an entrepreneur and start my own business. There's a meeting I want to go to, but would love you to come along so I can get your opinion."

Naturally, he agreed to come and he loaned me the joining fee. Meaning, I had said the right thing to the right person!

If I had said to him, "Dad, I have a meeting to go to for a business that might on first glance look less than conventional, and I can't get there as it's too far away - and I haven't got the money to invest either, so can you drive me there with your *American Express* card please?" – then I would have almost certainly said the wrong thing to the right person!

Here's my belief: if you are saying the wrong things to people, and explaining the business badly, then it doesn't matter whether you're speaking to the right prospect or not, people won't say "yes." By telling people that they were clearly not speaking to the right person, this simply gives them permission to not work on improving their skills or review what they're saying.

Another of these well-meaning but unhelpful phrases you will sometimes hear in network marketing is: "*If you throw enough mud at the wall, some of it will stick.*"

That phrase is incorrect on so many levels…

Let me start by saying, in the interest of being balanced and fair, it **is** actually true. If you throw a lot of actual mud at a wall then some of it will stick!

However, let me share with you why this is an unhelpful mindset if you are looking to build a large, profitable and long-term network marketing business.

Firstly, it's not mud – these are people you are dealing with. **Real** people who have genuine concerns and goals that your products will be able to help them; people who have financial, lifestyle and family dreams that they would like to achieve, with which your business opportunity could make a real impact. So the mud-throwing concept does not work when you see the people you are dealing with as mud.

What else? Well, if you have a wide-reaching, uncaring approach – and your team does the same – how long will it be before everybody has been spammed about what you do either in person or online? People will think they know about your product and opportunity, and will have formed a less-than-favorable opinion of your business and the entire profession.

The 'throwing mud at the wall' method goes completely against any relationship-building principles. Adopting this approach will mean they are unlikely to keep, or effectively work, a No-For-Now book. They are working purely on quantity, with no relationship or empathy established at any point.

One of the reasons we end up offering this well-meaning (but unhelpful) advice is because we learn that our team is feeling a bit despondent due to lack of results. As team leaders we encourage them to tell us exactly what it is they are saying to their prospects. What inevitably ends up happening though is that they tell us what they think they said (which may not have been what they actually said) - or they are a bit embarrassed so they tell us something that is far closer to the textbook or the training.

We hear their pitch and think that they are not that wide off the mark, so we assume that they just need to speak to more people. Hence, the suggestion to keep on throwing the mud, and assurances that they are speaking to the wrong person and therefore could never have said the right thing.

This process leaves us with no solution and we have team members who continue to get negative results, without any clear direction.

How can we help our teams to be more effective, or indeed, to get the support we need to ensure they win more often?

One way is to invite them to sit and make some calls with together, so we hear them in action. You can do this together in person or by listening in with some cool technology such as *Skype*, *Zoom* or *FaceTime*. These are free and easy to use - you simply dial in on your smartphone or tablet, and then listen while they make calls from another phone. You can also allow them to hear you make some of your calls.

Likewise with actual face-to-face presentations – why not shadow them on a couple and allow them to do the same with you?

If you are starting out yourself, then this is advice you can be mindful of when you start to build your own team – and in the meantime, you should ask your upline or a leader in your business to offer this type of support.

One often underused learning experience is when a handful of team members get together and have a "cake & calls," "cookies & calls," or even a "pizza & calls" session. Together, they blitz the phones, taking it in turns to make a call, and then share feedback in small groups.

Where distance or time is an issue, I know people often suggest role-play over the phone, particularly if someone isn't getting the results they desire.

The problem with this is that it can be too staged and therefore doesn't really address what is happening in a real-life situation. Therefore, as leaders, we can sometimes end up saying to people: "Don't worry – just keep doing what you're doing, and the results will come." This advice is well-meaning but not actually very helpful if we are only judging them on unrealistic role-play.

My solution to this issue is to suggest they download a simple recording app on their smartphone and record some calls. Encourage them to hit the record button during some live customer and business opportunity presentations. I ask people to start recording upon entering the house, or meeting their prospect in the coffee shop (or wherever they are), and not a few moments later when they begin the main topic of the presentation.

Why?

Quite simply, you need to hear the very important rapport-building stage to check whether they're ruining the presentation with what they are saying prior to it in the very beginning.

By inviting your team to work with you in this way you can then listen in and hear some live interactions and give much more meaningful, real and appropriate feedback.

Yes, it may take you half-an-hour to listen through a couple of recordings, and the same amount of time to offer feedback, but when this person goes on to become a star performer in your team, it will most definitely have been worthwhile.

While *The Prospecting Game* may well have helped you realize that getting a "no" is part of the journey, let's not believe that we can't improve our skills and approaches too.

> **If you are new to your business and still getting to grips with everything yourself, why not ask for this type of support and feedback from your sponsor or someone else in your leadership team?**

A few years back, I was working closely with Rachel, a lady in my network marketing business. She had been pretty successful with us but then all of a sudden she went on a run of twelve appointments without getting any sign-ups. Her ratios were generally much, much better than this and so the longer it continued, the more frustrated she became.

Frustration doubtless led to some desperation too, and as you may well have experienced, desperation is the easiest way to repel your prospects!

We had a chat about her situation and I suggested she record her next few presentations. Rachel wasn't thrilled with this concept, as she seemed to think that the problem was with the prospects, not herself.

I had a different view, and was thinking to myself: *"Mmmmm... well, who is at the scene of the crime every time? Maybe it's something **you're** saying?"*

She eventually agreed to record her next two appointments. I listened to the first one and it was perfect. I spotted one minor detail towards the end, but otherwise she was doing a great job and I was struggling to give any meaningful feedback.

I then listened to the second one and again, it was fantastic. In fact, I was worried she might ask to listen to some of my appointments and she would expose the fact that she was actually better than me. I was even wondering whether there was something else that was the problem – perhaps she had trodden in something on the way into the house and this was putting people off...

But then I got to the end of the second presentation, and there it was again, one little word out of place.

I listened again and at the end of the presentation, during her close, she said to them:

"So, would you like to give it a go, or…?"

I checked back to the first recording, and, there it was again.

"So…would you like to give it a go, or…?"

Just that one little word, **OR**!

What Rachel was doing, in effect, was leaving the close open. She was leaving a gap for the prospect to fill in their own response, which was giving them an excuse not to sign up!

So I asked her: "Why are you saying 'or' at the end of each presentation?"

Rachel looked surprised, "I'm not."

I produced the evidence! "Really? Ok, let's take a listen!"

We pressed play and forwarded to the end: "So would you like to give it a go, or…?"

She was shocked - she didn't know she was saying it, and was fairly sure this was a recent addition to her presentation. Probably true since she had previously been getting a much better ratio of positive outcomes. It had somehow slipped into her subconscious at some point and if I had not taken the time to listen to her, she may never have discovered it. She would have become increasingly frustrated, thrown in the towel and probably disappeared from our business.

My guess is that in the false environment of a role-play over the phone, for example, we would not have discovered this impediment.

Clearly this is another example that demonstrates if I had just sent her off with the reassuring words: "*You can't say the wrong thing to the right person, and you can't say the right thing to the wrong person*", I would not have actually helped her succeed.

This year, Rachel's business will turnover around $7 million in sales. It is fair to say that the hour or so I spent listening to and discussing her presentations with her was well worth the time!

Some people will encourage you to "throw mud at the wall," simply because they can't build relationships very well themselves. Others will say it to their teams in a well-meaning way, attempting to encourage them to keep going. Just like the '*you can't say the right thing to the wrong person*' line that we discussed above.

It is designed to make you feel better about rejection and that the problem lies with them not you, so you keep going. But this is an easy way out - working on skills, reviewing and evaluating what it is that you are saying, and receiving feedback will prove a much more effective way to ensure better results.

For a keynote speech I gave at the Network Marketing

Mastermind Event® in 2015, I prepared a short video that was aimed at revealing the real effects of throwing mud at the wall (it actually makes a mess!) and the trouble you can get yourself into by believing you can't say the wrong thing to the right person! Check it out – it's just a bit of fun: www.weslinden.com/mud

CHAPTER NINE

IT'S ABOUT THEM, NOT ME

I am a big believer that the language we use gives us clues as to the problems we may end up facing.

For example, when someone says to me:

"I just can't recruit."

"I need to find more people to sell my products to."

"I want to recruit lots of people into my team."

I hear someone who is focused on what *they* can get, and not how they can help other people.

One of my good friends in network marketing, Chris Williams, who authored and recorded the audiobook *Don't Just Dream It, Do It! Goal-Setting that REALLY Works for Network Marketers,* once said to me:

"When I used to spend lots of time thinking about who I could recruit into my team or sell my products to, I struggled to sponsor anyone. When I shifted my thinking and started figuring out who I could help with our products and who I could support to change their life for themselves and their family with our business opportunity, then suddenly my customer and sponsoring numbers went through the roof."

This had a profound impact on me. We spend a lot of time thinking about what we want or need for our next promotion or bonus. But if we shift the focus onto the prospect and how we can help them benefit, suddenly this mindset-shift and language-reframe will provide a more vibrant energy. The whole process becomes about the prospect. When they see that you are genuinely looking to help make a difference for them, they will be much more open-minded and warm to your approach.

This manner is essential when you are getting back in touch with people to find out if now is a better time for them to take a look at what you do. As Tom "Big Al" Schreiter often says, you won't have a great deal of joy if you simply call people or text them and say:

"Hi, so are you ready to become my customer now? I mean, after all, you're not getting any younger and your skin is wrinkling more every day/your health is getting worse every day/your weight loss issues clearly aren't going away/ you're poorer now than you were last time we spoke because you're still using that expensive utility company/you're still sending rubbish birthday cards/you're still drinking coffee that eats your insides..."

Or

"Hello, should we stop messing about and get you signed up to my team now so you can start making me some money, and get out of that dead-end job you're in?"

This type of abrupt approach won't work for anyone. You'll likely find they "switch off" very quickly, as it is clear you are looking at them with dollar signs in your eyes.

Find out how they are. Ask them how the house move went. How the new dog is settling in. How the kids' day out to the seaside was. All the conversation that you can recall (thanks to your No-for-Now book) from the last time you spoke to them, will show them that you are more than just a pushy salesperson.

Make people realize that you care. Show them that you are there, ready to support them when the time is right.

LEADER'S STORY:

Network marketing legend, international speaker and top author Tom "Big Al" Schreiter, knows a thing or two about building a successful team. Here's one of his stories about making friends for the sake of making friends:

"In 1982, I moved to Houston, Texas. One of the first friends I made was David. He loved talking with people. Since he was married with two small children, he kept a day job that paid a steady salary, plus a commission. His view of network marketing? Well, he already could increase his income by earning more commission with his day job, so he saw no reason to bother with network marketing.

In his day job, leads came to him. He didn't have to prospect. That was an advantage for David as he just left the Army and had recently moved to Houston. Network marketing just wasn't a good fit for him.

Well, over the years his children started to grow. David got remarried. And those secure sales jobs? They turned out to be not-so-secure. Time after time the companies changed the rules, lost their funding, closed, moved, changed ownership...and David kept moving from job to job.

Finally, in 1989, David had had enough. It was "his time" to join network marketing. And when he joined, he did fantastically.

Why? Because David now had six more years experience in talking to people. David had six more years where he had built new contacts in Houston and now had a list of people he could talk to.

And finally, David had a story. A great story. All David had to do was tell prospects about his frustration of moving from job to job, and how he was now going to finally take care of his future and make it secure.

Now, were David and I great friends during those years and years when network marketing just wasn't the right timing for him? Yes!

Not every friend or relative has to join network marketing. We are allowed to have good friends and relatives who have different interests and goals.

But here is what I later learned. During all those years that David didn't join my network marketing business, he was approached by other network marketers. Yet, he never joined them and their businesses.

I asked David: "Why didn't you join them?"

His answer? He said, "All those networkers only offered 'conditional friendships' - and that meant they only wanted to be my friend if I joined their business. As soon as I showed no interest in joining, they left. They weren't interested in me as a person. They were only interested in me as a possible commission check."

So have friends. Real friends. Not "conditional friendships" or a one-way agenda.

Friends join friends when the time is right for them."

There will be leaders or speakers who encourage you to recruit 50 people in 50 days, and tell you that this is the only way to succeed. This is not true. It's a good hook to sell courses, but if you ask any of the top network marketers how many people they have recruited on average per month, you'll find it's nothing like this.

Personally, I have introduced around 500 people into my network marketing business. Now, if I just leave you to chew on that number, you'll likely talk yourself into believing you can't do that. But then factor in that I have been active for over 18½ years, and work out how many months that is:

18½ years x 12 months = 222 months
500 people ÷ 222 months = 2¼ people per month!

I asked some of the world's top network marketers for their own figures –Art Jonak, Jordan Adler, Sarah Robbins, Eugene Hong, Steve Critchley, Robin & Cal Brooks, Orjan & Hilde Saele and Orrin Woodward. Only one of them said their consistent average was three a month. Most of them were averaging one to two per month, over their time in the business.

Of course, some months it may have been a few more than that, and other months less, however averaged out it is a far more attainable figure for most people.

And actually, my average is that I have introduced around two people a month.

> **Does that sound a little more doable now if you work on the skills and keep building your relationships?**

If all those leaders got to the top position in their businesses by introducing a couple of people a month on average, then surely you can do the same. Don't let anyone make you think that a consistent approach with one, two or three new distributors every month, can't work for you. Providing you can teach your new team members to get started and do the same, and they can then go on to sponsor too, your business will naturally grow.

If your prospects feel that your journey is more than just a mass exercise in gathering as many people as possible into your net as quickly as possible, you will succeed.

CHAPTER TEN

FISHING IN THE WRONG POND

We network marketers don't always make life easy for ourselves.

Often we invest far too much time chasing the wrong people. We do this for a number of reasons. This includes the fact that someone has been prepared to listen to us for a few minutes, or shown the slightest glimmer of interest in what we do; and often it's due to us setting our own boundaries as to the type of person we are prepared to speak to and we end up pitching that quite low.

I am a big advocate for not prejudging people, not least because, if prejudging prospects was the right thing to do, I would never have been introduced to this fantastic profession. After all, I turned up to my first opportunity presentation at a posh hotel wearing tracksuit bottoms, sneakers and a bomber jacket, with my hair all over the place (yes, I once did have hair!), and I hadn't shaved for several days. I was only twenty years old and a university student. I didn't sign up that night but my sponsor was good enough to take the time to follow-up with me a few days later. Anyone who prejudged would almost certainly not have taken me seriously.

Therefore, I say with absolute conviction: **do not prejudge people**. Well, let me clarify – we all prejudge people when we see them – this is a part of human conditioning. However, once you have prejudged them, offer them your products and opportunity anyway! However, also: decide where it's most effective to use your time.

If your prospect was barely awake during your presentation, didn't watch the online video you sent him, didn't turn up for the five opportunity presentations at which you arranged to meet, has never answered a call, and now crosses the street to avoid you, then they are telling you something.

If they haven't had a job for the past fourteen years, enjoy smoking, gambling and drinking all day, have all the cable channels, but have said they won't even be able to find the starter pack fee, then this really should be a clue that you should spend time concentrating on those who have more motivation.

Never deny anyone the opportunity, and who knows, that guy might change his ways and his focus at some stage in the future. But right now, he's probably not someone with whom you are going to build financial security!

Likewise with your product – when you spend time telling someone about how great your nutritional supplements are but they have been clear that they are pursuing as unhealthy a lifestyle as possible and have no intention of changing, then clearly they're not ready! When you've explained the wonderful savings you can offer them with their utility bills or their household items and they tell you that they are loyal to the big supplier because their next door neighbor's son used to work for them and they will never switch, then you should consider whether they deserve too much of your focus right now.

Again, this doesn't mean you can't drop them a polite line from time to time to check-in with them and see how they are doing, but ensure that this is not where you are pinning all your hopes.

CHAPTER ELEVEN

DESPERATION – THE BEST REPELLENT FOR NETWORK MARKETING SUCCESS

"I just can't believe they can't see it."

I was with a fellow network marketing leader recently who took a call from their sobbing teenage daughter. I couldn't help but eavesdrop on her advice.

She said to her daughter things like: *"When a new boy comes along you have to realize that you shouldn't focus solely on him and ignore all your other friends." "Try to be more relaxed about it – every new boy you meet is not 'the one' just because they look at you."*

This was followed by: *"There's plenty more boys in the world who will appreciate you,"* and: *"You can't stop dating and making new friends just because one or two guys have let you down."*

This made me think about the type of obsessive behavior that youngsters, and sometimes adults, display when they meet a new girl or boy, or they finally snare someone who shows them the slightest attention.

We all know instinctively that it is unhealthy and in the long term, counterproductive. Yet we often see that the guy or girl who is more *laissez-faire* in their attitude to dating is the one who has more success.

How many of us apply the same slightly obsessive behavior to our prospecting of new distributors and customers, or when we have a new team member join?

I think this is useful to keep in mind as we continue on our paths to financial success.

Desperation has a very obvious odor and prospects can sniff it out from a mile away. One of the things I hear so often from distributors is:

"I just can't believe they can't see it" or *"I really, really want it for them as they totally need it."*

I completely agree. There are plenty of people who just never see the value of our products or business opportunity, and there are many people in life that I know could really benefit from the opportunities our type of business offers. However, we have to resign from our desired role as Master Decision Maker and Life Organizer for the Entire Universe…

Our job is to share the information, keep people informed, check-in with them again from time-to-time, work with those who want to join as a distributor, and organize products for those who only wish to be a consumer

That being the case, when you are going through your No-for-Now lists and re-contacting people, be sure **not** to let them feel your frustration or desperation for them to become involved with your business, as this will repel rather than attract. Ultimately we are looking for people who themselves are looking – **we are searching for the volunteers, not the conscripts.**

It's also worth noting that the regularity of your exposures needs to be proportionate. Catching-up occasionally does not mean every 24 hours! That is another sure-fire way to entirely drive people out of your prospecting pipeline. Be respectful and appropriate with your exposures and you'll not cause prospects any stress.

I would suggest every three-to-six months for the warmer contacts who showed some interest, or those you have a good rapport with. For those who were a little less warm or you don't have a strong relationship with, I would recommend every six to twelve months.

Going back to the story with which I began this chapter, you'd be unlikely to tell your daughter to date anyone just because they know her name. And I doubt you would suggest she keeps calling the disinterested ones every fifteen minutes.

So, be sure to adopt a similar policy towards growing your own business!

CHAPTER TWELVE

IS IT WORTH THE EFFORT?

The problem was that Jamie couldn't make a decision.

In my early days, I had a conversation with a guy called Jamie. I showed him how our business opportunity worked and how it might benefit him. He worked nights as a taxi driver and I shared stories with him of other taxi drivers in our business, and how they had managed to regain some life balance since they had become involved with our business.

He had recently been blessed with the arrival of his second child and there was pressure from home to spend time with his family outside of his night shifts. I realized though that he could see the potential and he agreed to me keeping in touch from time to time.

So, every few months, I would schedule a call to him. Sometimes he would answer and other times he wouldn't.

> **Here's another tip for you – I normally don't leave a voicemail that asks the person to do anything, because 99% of the time they won't do it. If I leave a message asking them to call me back, and they don't, then over a period of time they will be embarrassed by this, almost certainly feel guilty, and thus try to avoid me in the future.**

When I am calling a No-for-Now prospect, if I can't get hold of them after a couple of attempts, rather than besieging them and having my number constantly on their 'missed calls' list, I will generally reschedule to call them again in another couple of months. There isn't going to be a hard-and-fast rule with this, and it depends on the prospect as to whether or not to leave a voicemail or not, but if I choose to do so then I simply say something like the following:

"Hi Jamie, it's Wes from XYZ – it was just a quick call to check-in again as we agreed I would do around this time, and see how things are going for you. I hope the football season ended well for your son's team and I will drop you a line again in

a couple of months. Look after yourself and we'll catch up soon."

The reason I leave a message like this is that it's friendly and upbeat. It is without pressure and it's not asking them to do anything. It is reminding them of the last conversation we had, but you will notice that there is no mention of business. It also leaves them feeling positive about me rather than negative, as they might have felt if I had left them a sales message on their voicemail.

Anyway, back to Jamie. During one call he mentioned to me that it was all right to call him in the evenings as he would be free to speak if he was sitting at the taxi stand waiting for his next fare. Every few months we would catch up and inevitably end up having a chat about whether now was a better time for him to take a proper look at our business opportunity and find out how we could work it around his other commitments. He would often ponder and waver but not commit, so I would say to him:

"That's okay, because timing is the most important thing. But would it be okay if we keep in touch from time-to-time, so I can find out how you're getting on, and let you know how we're doing?"

Years passed and we became quite good friends during our conversations, and I always felt he was worth investing time in. His family expanded and two children became three. He was feeling the financial and time pressures as he juggled his desire to provide for his dependents while having time off to enjoy them.

In total, we probably spoke around fifteen times, and after about nine years he finally said to me:

"Yes, let's get together."

He was ready to move off the rusty nail!

I suppose I'd better tell you the rusty nail story, as it'll be true for so many of your No-for-Now prospects.

Ruth had just moved into a new neighborhood. She liked her house and her environment, but there was one thing she didn't understand.

Her neighbor, Mr Pankhurst, had a dog that kept howling non-stop. Literally. Day in, day out.

"Awoooooo ... Awoooooo ..."

Initially Ruth thought the dog was just going through a phase, so she ignored the howls, thinking it would eventually stop.

But it didn't. The dog continued howling.

"Awoooooo ... Awoooooo ... Awoooooo ... "

One day passed. Nothing changed.

Two days passed. Still howling.

Three days - five days, then a week, then two weeks.

One month. Still howling, with no sign of stopping.

"Awoooooooo ...Awoooooooo ...Awoooooooo ...".

Finally, Ruth couldn't stand it any longer. One fine day, she walked over to Mr Pankhurst's house to see what was going on. Sure enough, there was the dog, sitting at the front porch, howling pitifully at whoever was walking by.

"Awoooooooo ... Awoooooooo ... Awoooooooo... Awoooooooo ... Awoooooooo ... Awoooooooo ..."

On the other hand, Mr Pankhurst was relaxing on his bench on the grass, leisurely reading his newspaper and sipping a cup of coffee..

Wondering what was going on, Ruth walked up to Mr Pankhurst.

"Hi Mr Pankhurst," Ruth said, "Is that your dog?"

"Which dog?" Mr Pankhurst replied before turning his head and glancing around. "Oh that. Yep he's mine."

Puzzled, Ruth asked, "Why does he keep howling?"

"Oh, that's because he's sitting on a rusty nail," Mr Pankhurst said.

"Sitting on a rusty nail?" Ruth gave the dog a bewildered

look. "Okay, so why doesn't he just get up off the rusty nail?"

"Well, Ruth," Mr Pankhurst paused and took a slow sip of his coffee before continuing. "Although the rusty nail hurts, it doesn't hurt enough for him to move yet."

So Jamie was finally finding his "rusty nail" too painful and was ready to move off it. We arranged to meet for coffee somewhere halfway between our homes.

When we got there, it had been so long since the last time I saw Jamie that I had lost quite a bit of weight – and my hair! I had also lost my glasses and now wore contact lenses. He didn't recognize me. To be fair, time hadn't been overly kind to Jamie – he was now sporting a few extra pounds and was wearing the stress of three children, coupled with his financial strains. Neither of us recognized the other and we ended up with the amusing situation of me calling his cellphone – him answering and us both realizing we were sitting almost next to each other!

We sat down and chatted. I ran through our presentation and Jamie agreed that now was the right time for him to get involved. He signed the forms and we set about helping him change the financial future for him and his family.

He was certainly keen. He would come to the events and was like a sponge for soaking up personal development. However, this wasn't translating into actual results. He managed to introduce a small handful of customers during his first eighteen months, which was certainly not going to change his financial plight, and made no major impact on our team's growth.

One could argue that my continued interest of Jamie with that many exposures, for several years, was clearly not worth it.

However, he did introduce a couple he met called Clive and Jan. They became distributors and they had a big "why" – they were approaching pension age and had lost a large amount of their savings and investments through a business deal that had backfired. They were in a hurry and were very keen to make the opportunity work. I built a relationship and friendship with them and over the following years they became leaders of a top-performing team in our business and were able to eliminate their financial worries.

Clive and Jan introduced a guy called Gary, a builder lacking in confidence, who, along with his wife Clare, it would be fair to say had some personal development to do. They undertook a great deal of personal development and worked on improving themselves. They took the business very seriously and soon they were able to take a three and sometimes four-day weekend as a family, rather than having to work five or six days a week.

Clive and Jan, Gary and Clare, the distributors, customers and all of the volume they brought to the business would never have happened if it hadn't been for Jamie, and my exposures to him over all that time. Many life pathways had been altered and sent in more positive directions because of their success. Despite the fact that Jamie never quite became the star himself, he discovered some stars.

Remember, it's not who you know, it's who **they** know that counts.

Was it worth the effort with Jamie? Of course – I gave him the opportunity to change his fortune, and he passed that opportunity to others.

By keeping in touch with people using an efficient No-for-Now follow-up system, and having patience with it, you never know who will join your business or become your best customer.

My good friend Sarah Robbins is a network marketing powerhouse and author of the book "Rock Your Network Marketing Business". She was speaking at the Mastermind Event in Orlando, and was passionate to explain that not all distributors have the goal of becoming a superstar. A truly selfless leader understands that fulfilling a small personal goal (a man just wanting an additional $50 per month for date night with his wife) is just as important as making a struggling single mom completely financially free with a 6 figure per month income.

She explains that we have to love people where they are, respect the level they're willing to go to (although we can always try and help them swim a little deeper) and not scare everyone off with talk of huge numbers if they're not ready to believe it is possible for them.

Sarah is very clear that we should celebrate every success equally, as each one is life-changing to those people. Some people need small goals (at first or always) because they don't believe they can achieve big money; or they have had so much programming to believe that money is evil that we need to be sure to help them where they're at.

CHAPTER THIRTEEN

IS REJECTION PERSONAL?

I have pondered for most of my network marketing career why distributors don't maintain ongoing contact with the people they share their products or services with. None of us enjoy rejection, but unless you have been overly pushy or incessantly stalked your prospect incessantly, the chances are that the process of someone not saying "yes" when you initially hope they might, is not really that painful.

Earlier in the book we discussed some of the reasons why people may initially put you off. Aside from the significant matter of timing, there could be many other reasons why the people you approach may not join straightaway.

"Let's see how you get on first" – I have never understood this one. Why would anyone make a decision about something based on how someone else gets on? If we all went about our life in this way, we would never get anything done. Imagine this:

Wife: "Breakfast is ready, dear."

Husband: "What are we having?"

Wife: "Bacon and two eggs overeasy"

Husband: "No – not for me."

Wife: "Why not?"

Husband: "Well, let me see how you get on first…"

What can you say if someone says this to you? I always try and focus the spotlight back onto them, it might go something like this:

YOU: *"So, if you were to consider getting involved with our business opportunity, what kind of extra income would make a difference to you?"*

PROSPECT: *"$500 per month."*

YOU: *"Great, we can certainly help you with that! We are all different and work at our own pace, so basing your decision whether to join on how I do wouldn't be a realistic comparison, but I can certainly help you achieve $500 per month, and there's no reason why we couldn't start working on that right away."*

What if they are saying they want to see how you get on with the product?

YOU: **"So, if you were to consider using these products, what result would you be looking for?"**

PROSPECT: "Weight loss/clearer skin/softer hands/lower electric bills/better nutrition/higher quality household products."

(Answer obviously depends on your product or service.)

YOU: "Great, we can help you with that! We are all different and have our own reasons for using these products, so basing your decision whether to use them or not on how I use them wouldn't be a realistic comparison, but I can certainly help you achieve the result you are looking for and there's no reason we couldn't start working on that right away."

I always love the words: 'We can help you with that'. It immediately tells the prospect that you are going to support them, and it's direct enough to be clear that you are serious about what you're saying.

This answer also explains politely that it's just not sensible or logical to compare your journey with theirs. I am not saying it works each and every time but it certainly is a way of responding that I have used with great success, and without saying what I really want to say (which is more aligned to the sarcasm in my bacon and eggs scenario above!).

There's also a question of vision – not everyone will have the foresight and vision to understand what it is that you do, or even why you are doing it.

LEADER'S STORY:

New York Times Best Selling Author and network marketing legend, Orrin Woodward, tells a fantastic story which sums up this scenario perfectly:

"Imagine you look out of the window and you see a dog jumping up and down, spinning around excitedly, barking, squealing and howling, doing backflips and somersaults, and you think to yourself 'Wow, that dog has lost its mind!'

Then, suddenly, you spot a rabbit, and the dog's behavior makes sense. Now you understand what the dog is getting excited about – you've seen the rabbit!

Well, it's the same with your network marketing business – you enjoy the products, you love the opportunity, and your friends see you jumping up and down with excitement, spinning around with glee, and they think you may have gone crazy!

However, they can't 'see the rabbit' – you can, but for now they can't. That doesn't mean they won't in the future. And it doesn't mean the rabbit doesn't exist. It does – they just can't see it - yet."

There's a host of other reasons why people may not say "yes" right away, aside from the timing not being right for them:

*In some cases they may be quite comfortable and living a great life, or indeed they may have their head in the sand, and they're not prepared to look beyond where they currently are – but that doesn't mean this won't change over time.

*Alternatively they may be skeptical because what we do in network marketing is currently a non-traditional way to buy products or to build a business. People are still used to buying all their goods from the local store or earning money from a 9-5 job.

*It could be that they are actually trying to protect you - maybe from failure if they have a 'glass half-empty' mentality or from disappointment if the business doesn't work out.

*It could be they are trying to protect themselves – often people who have little faith or confidence in their own ability do not want to put their head above the parapet. Offering them an opportunity to build their own business, where the result is so obvious for others to see, is something that undoubtedly terrifies some folk.

*We also have to understand that there are people who are challenged when the status quo is interrupted. It can be very unsettling when they see or hear that someone might be doing something that may elevate them financially, socially and spiritually above their current standing.

*What about this as a possibility then? Maybe **we** were the problem! Maybe we distastefully shouted about our new business too loudly. Maybe they couldn't escape it - in person, on the phone, by text, or on *Facebook*, *Twitter*, *Instagram* or *WhatsApp*. All they could hear was how this amazing shake will help them lose 20lbs in five minutes, or how this opportunity will allow them to become a millionaire in the next 30 days while doing nothing! That is terribly off-putting (as soon as you notice your team doing this, STOP them immediately).

*And finally, there's one fact that you won't like, but it's indisputable, and that is that some people will never ever be right for your products, your services or your business opportunity. We must understand that this is perfectly okay! Not everyone has to like what you are doing and not everyone has to see what you can see. Many people will have perfectly happy lives without ever being involved with network marketing or consuming your products!

CHAPTER FOURTEEN

YOUR STORY – THE TRUTH IS GOOD ENOUGH

"How can I recruit when I haven't got a Ferrari?"

One of the most common challenges people present themselves as they are starting and growing their network marketing business, is that they don't have the material and financial proof to present themselves as successful.

This view is understandable, but misguided. What we are doing here is allowing ourselves to get caught up in the 'mystique' of the traditional success stories in network marketing, and having forgotten about the real world.

Let me explain.

At the time of writing this book, a recent survey* has shown that the average disposable monthly income, after all bills are paid, for an individual in the UK (based on UK figures and exchange rate at time of print), is $315. However, 25% of the population have $70 or less each month and 1 in 11 people (4.5 million British adults) have less than $15 a month left over after they have paid all their essential bills.

18-24 year olds have well below the average in disposable income – just $245 per month.

Only 13% of people said they had more than $700 left over each month in disposable income.

So what would that suggest to you? Most of the people that you know, work with, or come into contact with, are living on a tight budget. Even those you think are well off. Indeed, for many of them, flashy cars, mansions and Rolex watches are not their immediate priority, and it could be argued that currently the idea of achieving such riches wouldn't be believable for them.

Therefore, your stories as you are growing your business are exceptionally relevant and powerful. Tales of people working full-time on their jobs, but fitting their direct sales business into the nooks and crannies of their day and achieving some much-needed additional income are really compelling.

The story of stay-at-home moms working in between school runs from the kitchen table, to build up a business that will help support the family, is inspiring.

The story of the dad who can work a four-day week now, rather than five, and can pick his kids up from school thanks to his part-time business, is very powerful.

A home-based income that is helping individuals and families enjoy additional luxuries and an extra night out each month – this is the difference between merely existing and enjoyable living for many, many people, as the statistics above show.

Don't be afraid to share real stories, either your own or people who have been in your business a little longer – there's no need to lie or exaggerate. Keep them authentic and keep them believable.

I was recently at a barbeque for some team members and began chatting with a guy called Derek, who, along with his wife Ayelet, were working our network marketing business in their spare time.

Derek is a teacher and Ayelet is a mobile hairdresser. Derek was explaining that he was having difficulty sharing the products or the business opportunity with people not really understanding why he was building the business in his spare time, particularly if they knew that he worked as a teacher.

So he found himself disregarding his own story.

Instead, he was speaking about the riches and significant wealth trappings that were possible, and that his leaders were benefiting from, and although he was getting customers, he was struggling to introduce team members.

I realized that he needed help constructing his story in a brief and believable manner, so that people could instantly see why he was doing this alongside his day-job. He could then use this story at the beginning of his product and business opportunity presentations as part of an introduction. Ideally it would work for people he knows, or those he doesn't know, and whether he discusses the business opportunity or the products. So here's what we came up with:

""As you know, I'm a teacher, and I really enjoy it. However, the job is becoming more and more stressful, and I don't want to carry on like this forever. So the reason I have started this business in my spare time, from home, is that in five years' time, I can leave teaching, and help Ayelet give up her work as a hairdresser. Then we can have more time together to travel, which is our passion. Anyway, let me show you how our products can help you/let me show you how the money works."

If you time this, you'll see it will take about 25 seconds to deliver. I would recommend that your story not last much longer than 20 to 30 seconds, because otherwise people will switch off. They don't need your life story!

This only gives a brief overview, explains who he is, why he is doing it, and what his goals are. It is palatable for anyone and is truthful, but also humanizes the situation, stops him sounding like a salesman, and prevents them sitting around thinking: "What is Derek up to, I thought he was a teacher?'

Here are a couple of other examples from people who I have helped construct their own story:

Business Owner

"As you know, I have my own restaurant business, and I love what I do, but the local main street businesses have been hit hard with parking regulations. So the reason I am doing this business in my spare time, from home, is so that whatever happens with the restaurant over the coming years I will be able to afford to put Tristan through university. Anyway, let me show you how our products can help you/let me show you how the money works."

Frustrated Employee

"As you know, I work 9-5 for one of the big insurance companies, and, to be honest, it's not my passion and the money isn't great. So the reason I am doing this business in my spare time, from home, is so that over the next couple of years I can have additional money for skiing holidays which I love, and at some stage look to quit my job altogether. Anyway, let me show you how our products can help you/let me show you how the money works."

Retiree

"You won't know this but I retired from nursing a few years ago, and although I am enjoying retirement, I miss the buzz of working. So the reason I am doing this business in my spare time, from home, is for the challenge and to help other people, while topping up my pension at the same time. Anyway, let me show you how our products can help you/let me show you how the money works."

Stay-at-Home Mom

"As you know, I became a mom a year ago, and Noah is my priority every day, but I am missing out on some of the little luxuries that we used to be able to afford. Since starting this business in my spare time, working around my baby's day, from home, I now have my own business that helps to pay for all those extras we want as a family. Anyway, let me show you how our products can help you/let me show you how the money works."

Chasing Dreams

"As you know, I work as a real estate agent right now, and I love what I do. My dream is to get a property in the Hawaii but my salary just won't stretch to that. So the reason I am doing this business in my spare time, from home, is so that over the next few years, we can have three months off over the winter to enjoy some sunshine. Anyway, let me show you how our products can help you/let me show you how the money works."

When putting your own story together, it needs to be compelling and real. When it's authentic and true for you, people will believe it, rather than pie-in-the-sky predictions.

Let's give you an example of the basic format to put your own story together:

Step 1

As you know, I'm a_____

OR

What you won't know is I'm a_____

Step 2

…and I really enjoy it,

OR

…and I am really not enjoying it,

Step 3

…but_____
_____
_____

Insert the part of your situation that you want to change:

e.g. My dream is…but my salary just won't cover that; the hours are really anti-social; I miss the buzz of working; I'm looking for a challenge; it's not my passion; I am missing out on some of the little luxuries that we used to be able to afford; the work is really boring; my job is becoming more and more stressful…

These are just a few generic examples, so make sure you say something that is relevant to your own situation.

Step 4

The reason I've started this business in my spare time, from home....

(This bit is **key** – use of the words "*spare time*" and "*from home*" tells the prospect that they could do this also and having a job or a busy life is no obstacle.)

Step 5

...is so that in ___ years' time, I/we can _____

_____

_____

Here you can give them a realistic timeline for your plans, and then where you see the future taking you with your network marketing business

e.g. We can have three months off over the winter to enjoy the sunshine; help Ayelet give up her work as a hairdresser; so we can have more time together to travel, which is our passion; I can have my own business that helps to pay for those extras we want as a family; is for the challenge and to help other people, while topping up my pension at the same time; whatever happens with the restaurant over the coming years I am able to afford to put Tristan through university ...

Again, you need to insert whatever is authentic and real for your situation.

I recommend that you take some time now to ensure you have your own story ready to tell, one that is relevant to you.

This saves you mumbling and tripping over your words; it saves you having to compensate by pretending to be an expert, talking about intricate product details, and sounding and looking like a salesman; it humanizes the whole process, and actually gives your prospect an opportunity to put themselves in the picture and think about what lifestyle changes they could make in their spare time working from home.

You want the people you are with to believe, "I could do that too."

(To download and print worksheets to help you with this exercise go to www.weslinden.com/support)

But what if they ask: "How much are you earning?"

Uh-oh! One of the biggest challenges in the mind of a new distributor is this question. You know what though? It never changes. Having reached the top position in my business, you'll understand that I have nothing to complain about when it comes to my monthly income. However, if someone asks me, I feel as bothered by answering today, as I did when I was starting up.

Why? Because I realized that it's hard, if not impossible, to ever say the right figure. You see, if you tell them that you earned $40 last month, because you only just started – that won't be good enough. If you tell them you're earning $40,000 per month, then for most people (who don't earn that in a year), that figure is not a believable or an achievable one (at least not straightaway). It's very rare you'll ever win answering this question, whatever amount you quote.

I would avoid the smart answers that we find amusing or clever as a network marketer, but to the public, just seem evasive or condescending (or unclear) – for example:

"I don't know, they haven't stopped paying me yet," or "You wouldn't believe me if I told you."

Instead, I encourage new team members to take a different approach when trying to answer this question, if it should come up. Here are some examples of how to deal with it:

Q: *How much are you earning then?*
A: *Well, I've only just started so it's not giving me a full-time income yet, however, it's helping me pay my mortgage each month, which is really useful. What would you be looking to earn from this business?*

OR

Q: *How much are you earning then?*
A: *Well, I've only just started taking it seriously, so it's not giving me a huge income yet, however it's covering the cost of an extra holiday each year, which is fantastic. What would you be looking to earn from this business?*

OR

Q: How much are you earning then?

A: Well, I'm putting a lot of time into building it up at the moment so it's still early for me. However, it's covering some of the bills at home, which is great. What would you be looking to earn from this business?

OR

Q: How much are you earning then?

A: Well, I've only just started committing more time to it so I'm still working at the hospital; however, it's giving us the money to give Christine horseback-riding lessons, which she loves. What would you be looking to earn from this business?

OR

Q: How much are you earning then?

A: Well, we've been involved a little while now and put in lots of our spare time in the early days, so I've now been able to leave my job, which is fantastic. What would you be looking to earn from this business?

Let's look at how we can help you to create your own answer.

You will notice that none of the examples above boast of pie-in-the-sky fantasies. In the long term, hype doesn't help. So if you are asked the question, then my belief (as a Brit!) is that this is personal information and I am not going to answer it with hype.

Therefore, I believe the way to answer is to start by positioning your involvement appropriately and your current situation (e.g. *"Well, I've only just started so it's not giving me a full-time income yet..."*). This immediately disarms any suspicion that you are trying to hype your success.

Next, you should share how this is assisting you (e.g. *"however, it's helping me pay my mortgage each month, which is really useful"*). In that example, there is a difference between saying that your business is actually paying for your mortgage and helping you pay for it. Obviously, don't use this example if you're only earning $20 because it is still the beginning and your mortgage is $800!

You need to tailor this around your own relevant situation. Even if your income is fairly small currently, you can still legitimately say that this is paying towards something meaningful, whether that is certain bills, family expenses or fun times out.

You need to construct your own answer that is authentic and true for you:

Question: *How much are you earning then?*

Answer:

Step 1:   *Well, I've_____*

(e.g. only just started; just started taking it seriously; been working quite hard in my spare time; been involved a little while now and put in lots of our spare time in the early days, etc.)

Step 2:   *...so I'm_____*

(e.g. still working at the hospital; not getting a huge income yet; not full-time yet; building it up; now able to leave my job, etc.)

Step 3:   *...however it's_____*

(e.g. giving us the money for Christine to have horseback-riding lessons; covering some of the bills at home; covering the cost of an extra holiday each year, etc.)

Step 4:   *which_____*

(e.g. she loves; is great; is fantastic; is really helping, etc.)

Step 5: *What would you be looking to earn from this business?*

Please note: If you have just started and haven't yet earned anything, at Step 3, you can say: "so the plan is..." instead of: "however it's..." therefore allowing you to share your initial goals.

(To download and print worksheets to help you with this exercise go to www.weslinden.com/support)

The question regarding what you are earning is normally more about the other person than it is about you. Essentially, they want to know what they can earn, and are attempting to use your success as a barometer for themselves.

Step 5 allows you to ease them away from talking about you and what you're earning (which is frankly irrelevant, since what you earn is based on your efforts, commitment and skills, and they may put in much more time and effort than you, or much less) and over to them and what they actually want.

It's true to say that someone with an employee mentality will want to understand the remuneration so we shouldn't appear evasive or full of hype – however this is our chance to show people that this is not a time for money job, but instead a business that can make a difference to lifestyles at many levels (from getting out of debt money, to extra disposable income, to serious choice to financial freedom.)

By spending time working out how best to present your story and success, and then practicing your delivery, it will become natural for you to share with others and this will make a big difference to the reaction you get.

Always speak the truth – be realistic, achievable, friendly and in keeping with what they know about you, but aspirational and authentic, and you'll find that the truth really is good enough.

*Research from budgeting account provider Think-Money, sourced via www.financialreporter.co.uk

CHAPTER FIFTEEN

PROSPECTING TIPS – GETTING TO MORE YESES

It's a treasure hunt.

Surely you wouldn't spend time searching for gold only to find a pebble and then spend hours trying to convert it into treasure? By the same token, avoid spending too much time trying to change the mind of someone who isn't ready right now. As discussed extensively in previous chapters, this is a process of sifting through and timing is the most important thing, however eager we are to progress instantly.

When a waiter goes to a table to check if everyone is okay, or would they like another drink, if people say: "No thanks," does he run away and squeal? Or does he leave them to enjoy their meal, and come back later to ask again if the time is right?

Just keep adding people to your list and approaching new people. Then you'll become much more relaxed about the process as inevitably, positive responses will come, and at the same time, you'll have lots of people to add to your No-for-Now list to reapproach in the future.

I've spent eighteen years learning the wrong ways and those negative experiences will guide you to the right ways! Let me share some top prospecting tips with you now:

Prospecting Tip #1 – QUICK!

It's easier to be in a rush!

For example, if you are prospecting someone you know and are looking to make an appointment or get them to a presentation, it's easier to avoid too much chatter and questioning, so open the call with these words:

"It's just a quick call…"

That way, if they start firing hundreds of questions, you are able to say to them: *"Well, as I mentioned it's just a quick call, because I'm heading out the door in a moment, but let's get together for twenty minutes so I can show you a presentation – is Tuesday or Wednesday better?"*

For cold prospects who you meet out and about and you want to give some information and set a time to follow-up:

"I'm in a rush right now…"

"I don't have much time to discuss it right now…"

Prospecting Tip #2 – LOVE!

Being nice works well! I always like to look for the positive in people and think the world is a better place when we move through it behaving courteously and with a smile on our face. Try it – it will certainly lift your mood.

Likewise, I know a lot of people are starved of compliments, but negatives are freely shared. There is lots of good research (including from the prominent professor Dr. John Gottman) that people need between three and seven positive comments to overcome one negative, so why shouldn't we play our part in supporting this?

If I am speaking to someone I know, I find that complimenting them is much more likely to make them warm to me, and it's also a great opening:

"You're a successful businessman…"

"You've got a good business brain on you…" "You're a smart guy…"

"You know lots of people…"

"You've got a great energy and a positive mind…" "You're always open-minded…"

"I always trust your judgment and opinion…"

Compliments also work well with people you don't know:

"You've got a great way with people…"

"I have to tell you, your service is great…"

"Thank you for your help today – it's because of you that I come here rather than that place up the road…"

"You're so good at what you do, I hope they pay you well…"

Prospecting Tip #3 – PROPOSAL!

It's important to realize that when you want to show someone your opportunity or products, different approaches will work for different people, depending on the situation, what you know of them already, and what your relationship is with them.

There is definitely not a "one for all" that works with everyone, so it's worth getting to grips with different styles of approach so that you can tailor what you say around the person you are speaking to:

"I've just started a new business and I really value your opinion. Can we get together for twenty minutes so I can run it past you?"

"I've just started a new business which I am really excited about, and I think there'll be some benefits in it for you. Let's get together so I can show you face-to-face."

"I have come across a really exciting business and I wanted you to be one of the first people I speak to about it."

"If I could show you how to increase your income, without it affecting your job, would you be open to finding out more about it?"

"With your people skills you could make a lot of money in our business. Are you open to other ways of making money alongside what you do right now?"

"I appreciate that what I'm doing in my spare time from home won't be for you – but I know you're well connected, so can I show you briefly what we do? Then if anyone springs to mind who you think might be interested, you can let me know."

"I was thinking about what you said earlier regarding (not retiring until you're 70/not getting away enough/ being overworked/looking for a change/paying for the kids' swimming lessons) and I think I might have something that could help you achieve that…"

"Are you studying or do you work here full-time?"

(I find this is a great one in restaurants, cafes or retail – even if someone looks far older than university or college age, they will normally find it amusing that you thought they might be younger, and inevitably, no matter what age, they will then explain their situation. In most cases with this question, they will tell you

122

something about their situation that could give you a door opener. i.e. "I was made redundant recently; not much work in the field I want; part-time job for extra money; fits in around kids; used to be in the Army; looking to become a teacher next year; I'm an actor.")

"Our business is actually expanding in your area right now, and we're looking for open-minded people who like the idea of building another stream of income without it affecting what they do already."

"I'm looking at setting up a new business from home and need a couple of people to take a look and see if it looks as good as I think it does."

"I know you know lots of people but my business is expanding in the area and I'm wondering if you know any enthusiastic and ambitious people who live there?"
("YES!")
"Great – can you give me their contact details or connect me with them on Facebook?"

You'll notice that some of these are quite direct; some of them are more indirect. Some will work better with people you know, some will work better with those you don't know.

The words are mostly interchangeable between the different versions and they are by no means exclusive. Your leaders may have others they can suggest too. These are just a few to be working on, and by all means, build your own. It's important you know what you want to say so you can deliver with confidence and you can prospect without stumbling over your words.

Prospecting Tip #4 – NEXT STEP!

It's really important to establish the next step – and that means either getting some information into their hands, or a presentation planned.

Here are some examples, and again these will interchange depending on the person and the situation:

"Here's my card – there's a link to a brief presentation – are you able to take a look at it tonight or over the weekend?"

"If I get you some information across, would you be able to take a look at it today or tomorrow?"

"Are you near a computer or smartphone right now?" (**"YES!"**)
"Great – I'll send you over a link to a short video."

"We've got a webinar planned this week which will explain everything – I'll send the link straight over."

"Do you prefer to read text or watch video?"
(I like this one because they can only really give you a positive response – plus you find out what format is best for them to be given some information.)

"Let me give you this – it will explain more about what we do."

"We need to sit down for twenty minutes so I can show you how it works."

"We've got a presentation on Thursday night which I will tell you all about it."

Prospecting Tip #5 – DATE!

Finally, we need to agree upon a time or date to either meet or follow up. I don't encourage you to finish an invite without knowing and recording the follow-up in your diary.

I also advise against settling for someone saying: *"Oh, I will give you a call when I have looked at it,"* because I can assure you, they usually never get around to it!

Which one you use depends on what you have said to them in Tip #4, of course.

"Wednesday or Thursday, when is best for you?"

"Do you think you will have looked at it by the weekend?"
("YES!")
"Great, I'll give you a call then – Saturday or Sunday, what's best for you?"

"I'll pop back to answer any questions – is Monday or Tuesday better for you?"

The basic five-step principle behind what I have shared with you here is this:
Quick – Love – Proposal – Next Step – Date

You need to be quick and you should give them some **love**, i.e. pay them a compliment. Next you share the **proposal**. At this stage you keep it brief but get some information into their hands or invite them to a presentation for the next step. After that you fix a date to follow-up or meet.

When following-up, I prefer not to ask if they have questions. Instead, I always like to ask: "*What did you like best?*" as this provokes a positive response and forces their brain to focus on the part that appealed to them most, which then gives you clues about how best to move forward.

For example: "*I sent you that video link yesterday – what did you like best about it?*"

"*So based on the presentation you saw tonight, what did you like best about it?*"

If you're looking to add prospects to your lists, read this chapter over and over. I'm confident if you commit this five-step principle to memory (**Quick – Love – Proposal – Next Step – Date**), you won't be short of a way to prospect in your warm or cold market, either directly or indirectly.

CHAPTER SIXTEEN

THE SECRET NO-FOR-NOWS

There's a whole list of "No-for-Now" folk that you haven't even thought of yet.

For those of you who have already started building your customer base and your team, your No-for-Now list is much bigger than you realize.

> **Have you ever introduced someone into your business, either as a customer or a distributor, and then you drop them a line only to find they've stopped answering your calls?**

Sadly it happens sometimes, and when you do finally get to speak to them you realize that they're not focused on your products, services or business. Maybe they've been spooked by another person's opinion.

Whatever the case may be, they have become a No-for-Now themselves. They just happen to have a customer account number or a distributor code.

My experience tells me that there are many people who love the idea and the concept, and they jump in either as a customer or a distributor. However, other priorities get in the way, and their excitement slowly dissipates. Then they either become dormant or inactive, or may even quit the business. This doesn't mean they can't or won't do it in the future, it just means the time wasn't right for them.

Therefore, I recommend you keep this in mind and factor these people into your No-for-Now list too, for occasional contact. You'll need to use some intuition with this – if someone unequivocally doesn't like your product, service or business opportunity, you'll pick this up from them fairly quickly. However, there will be those who want the door left ajar, but for whom the timing isn't quite right.

You will be amazed how often, when you reach out to an inactive distributor, they'll say: *"I'm glad you phoned – I have been thinking about starting up again but was embarrassed to call as I didn't want you to think I was going to waste your time."*

A catch-up can be just that – no huge pressure, just checking in to see if now is a better time for them to get involved again. It could be an invite to a company event, or team social; it could be to update them with some new announcements or incentives.

I mentioned Gary and Clare earlier on. After a decent start, life got in the way. Family issues, the sad loss of a parent, and pressures from work all led to inactivity in their network marketing business. I kept in touch with them from time to time, and eventually the time was right for them to get involved again.

Gary often shares in hindsight how, when I called them, my first words were: *"How's it going mate?"* rather than saying, *"Why aren't you working harder on your business – do you want to fail?"*

As frustrating as it may be, the timing is about them, not you. Embrace that and you will win.

LEADER'S STORY:

Steve Critchley is the top-earner in his network marketing business, but when he first started, he was fitting his network marketing business around a full-time job in the day and a part-time job in the evening. However, Steve quickly realized the value of maintaining long-term relationships:

"Our entire business is about building relation-ships that last. I have learned that we shouldn't spend too long trying to assess the financial value of each person we connect with. You never know what you might learn from them, who they might refer you to, or how you may be able to help them at some point. Even if they're not ready for your network market ing business when you first talk to them about it, it doesn't mean they won't be in the future.

"Around 2003, I met a new guy named Craig who had joined our opportunity and he was hungry for it. He started to push forward with the business and was having fun and getting results.

"Have you ever noticed that sometimes life can throw some curveballs at you? Craig was soon to become entwined in life challenges as his marriage was coming to an end, causing him some financial headaches.

"Craig was forced to concentrate more on his full-time employment and the stress of his home situation didn't leave him feeling particularly empowered to grow his network marketing business.

"We kept in touch but I could see his heart wasn't in it, and gradually, he stopped answering my calls, and eventually he ended his involvement with our business. The buzz had gone for him.

"I have always realized that timing is vital when we are building a long-term, sustainable income, so while Craig was gone for now, that didn't mean he was gone forever. Plus, I liked Craig. He was a character and we had become friends. I wanted life to turn out well for him whether or not he was in my business.

"Every few months I would give Craig a call for a catch-up. Sometimes he would answer, sometimes he wouldn't. Sometimes he would call me back and sometimes he wouldn't. It didn't matter. All that mattered, from my point of view, was that we kept the lines of communication open.

"Ten years later, life had changed for Craig and he was in a much happier place in his life. He still had that urge to create a residual income and on one occasion we happened to speak at the right time. He was ready to get started again.

"Back he came with a renewed optimism and enthusiasm that this time he would see it through. Three years from that point, he has achieved various promotions, holiday incentives and top performer awards, and his business continues to grow.

"The lesson? It didn't take much effort to keep in touch with Craig every few months and it turned out to be worthwhile, just for our friendship, but also for him to feel wanted enough to swallow his pride, rejoin the business and start all over again.

"But the real lesson? Craig wasn't the only person I was reconnecting with.

"There are many others who I maintained contact with, and still do; some for whom the time became right, others for whom it hasn't.

"Rob was another interesting story and someone else I introduced to our business. He was a car washer, we got on well, and he got off to a great start. However, after that Rob did very little for the following six years.

"I regularly stayed in touch, and one day asked how his hands were doing as it was an extremely cold day outside. We chatted for a while, and I eventually learned that this question about his hands was a turning point for Rob. He later told me his hands were sore and full of cuts from the hard, manual work outdoors cleaning cars.

"Rob is now one of my top leaders. He told me recently that it was the fact that I regularly kept him updated - without harassing him – simply taking a genuine interest in his well-being, that was the turning point for him.

"It's good that I stayed in touch!

"To become a top networker, it's important that I keep in touch with people I connected with.

"Some prospects I spoke to never joined in the first place; some joined and didn't quite make it work but kept their position; and some joined and quit.

"I can't remain in touch with every single one of them of course – there is a natural process of self-selection. If someone never, ever answers my call, or when they do they, make it obvious that they don't want to speak to me, then they are likely to fall down my priority list.

"So while Craig and Rob are two of many success stories from this consistent approach, there were also people who still haven't become a customer or a distributor.

"Do I lay awake at night worrying about those who haven't joined my team?

"No, I concentrate my thoughts and efforts on those who said 'yes!'"

CHAPTER SEVENTEEN

IS IT A PYRAMID?

Stav: "Nice jersey."

Neil: *"It's a sweater."*

Stav: *"Oh, sorry – I thought it was a jersey!"*

Neil: *"No – it's a sweater. Don't call it a jersey. Jerseys are uncool – a sweater is totally different. Don't you know anything?"*

#Awkward!

Occasionally, people may ask you about your business and say: "Is it a pyramid?"

Relax.

I have some good news for you.

In most cases it is not an insult, discourtesy or a slur.

This is how I recommend you respond to this question, with confidence and posture:

Mandy: "Is it a pyramid?"

Stephen: "That's an interesting question – when you say '**pyramid**', what do you mean specifically?"

Note that in the answer, this is said without fluster, angst or aggression. It's simply a question back, in response to their question.

Why? You need to know what **they** mean by 'pyramid', before doing what many network marketers do, barking off a flippant or argumentative response.

If you find that people are asking or even suggesting that the business is a pyramid scheme on a regular basis, then you need to get help from a respected upline. I would say that usually any negative responses you are experience are a direct result of something you are saying to them.

On the rare occasion you get asked this, what I have also found is that nine times out of ten they do not mean anything negative by it. It's simply that they don't know what else to call our type of business.

It may well be that they have heard of businesses where you can work from home in your spare time, and build a recurring income. They may have also heard of businesses where you can build a team of friends and family as well. Who knows, they may even have had someone they know talk to them about one before.

This doesn't mean that they're being rude about your business; it just means they don't have a descriptive term to use.

So when you reply with your question as shown above, you normally find the response is something like this:

Mandy: "Is it a pyramid?"

Stephen: "That's an interesting question – when you say 'pyramid', what do you mean specifically?"

Mandy: "Oh you know, one of those businesses where you work from home alongside your job selling products for a company and you can introduce other people into a team as well, in a kind of pyramid shape, so you earn a bit off what they sell, and then you earn a bit off what their team does as well?"

Mandy's response here is not word-for-word what you will hear, but I tend to find it is something along those lines. What you learn from this, is that they simply don't have the correct word to describe the business you are in, as opposed to being negative.

If you go back to the start of this chapter, to the conversation between Stav and Neil, this is a little more like the type of exchange network marketers have when faced with the pyramid question. They are instantly defensive and confrontational.

The result is that a barrier forms between you and your prospect. They suddenly start wondering why you are so defensive and it ruins the flow of the conversation.

So here's how I recommend you respond:

Mandy: "Is it a pyramid?"

Stephen: "That's an interesting question – when you say 'pyramid', what do you mean specifically?"

Mandy: "Oh you know, one of those businesses where you work from home alongside your job selling products for a company and you can introduce other people into a team as well, in a kind of pyramid shape… so you earn a bit off what they sell, and then you earn a bit off what their team do as well?"

Stephen: "Oh yes, that's kind of how it works… anyway, what would you be looking for from this type of opportunity/anyway can you see how the products could help you?"

Why get stuck on terminology when they don't even know that the pyramid description could be seen as detrimental? Instead, just agree and move them on to discussing what's in it for them.

If we go back to the conversation between Stav and Neil, Neil ruined the mood with his snappy response. Don't be like Neil – be like Stephen, who carried on the conversation seamlessly.

CHAPTER EIGHTEEN

DREAM - STRUGGLE - VICTORY

"I can't get people to join."

I started this book with an overview of the type of conversation I have numerous times a week with people who are struggling to get people to join their business, or try their products and services.

Most of the angst they face comes from not having confidence and posture in their communications. This nearly always arises from a lack of results.

A lack of results comes from not taking the time to learn some basic conversational skills about speaking to prospects.

Additionally, distributors fail to understand the importance of relationship-building, ignoring the need to follow-up and keep in touch regularly. Finally, there's a lack of regard for the basic rules of marketing.

All this leads to their growing desperation, which results in casualties within our network marketing business.

If this applies to you, I believe you now have some tools to help build your business with confidence and posture, and you can throw desperation out of the window! This will make you more attractive to your prospects for when the time is right for them.

If you are now leading a team, you can be sure there are some people who are marching around without the necessary skills or feeling nervous about their business and not getting results. They need your help. We need to support them so they can relax and enjoy the journey to network marketing success.

I would hazard a guess that it took me longer than many of the success stories in your business to reach the top position in my company.

> **However, my attitude has always been that I am swimming in my lane and they are swimming in theirs.**

My recommendation to you is that you adopt the same approach. Don't obsess over who is going faster than you; who is making more money; who is recruiting more people – you didn't join your network marketing business to beat those people, so why is it so important now?

Swim in your lane...

Enjoy your journey...

Learn the skills…

Practise them…

Do it consistently...

Relax…

Make friends for the sake of making friends…

Help others…

Develop your posture…

The results will follow.

Fact.

But what is also a fact is this: Wherever your finishing post is, the road there begins with a dream – a goal and a vision - because you want something more.

That road is not straight. The road has potholes, obstructions, distractions and diversions.

From dream to victory you have to accept that there's going to be some struggle along the way. The struggle sorts the achievers from those who just think about it. The struggle sorts the folk who achieve their victory from those who nearly did. The struggle separates those who are able to change the direction of their own life and the lifestyle opportunities for their family, from those who scamper off at the first hurdle.

It goes like this: Dream – Struggle – Victory.

This was the entire theme at a recent Network Marketing Mastermind Event® for a reason. Because that's the way it is!

We can't get the victory without the struggle.

With that in mind, I wish you every success in building your network marketing business. I won't wish you luck though, because it's not down to that.

I urge you to revisit this book again and again in the future, as your experiences will give some messages a whole different meaning.

When you find a team member who is struggling with rejection, what to say, posture, confidence, desperation and staying on track, plus the other tips *The Prospecting Game* has discussed, you may wish to recommend that they read a copy also.

It's my pleasure to share this knowledge and these tips with my colleagues in the network marketing profession. Together we can all dream our dreams, battle through our struggles, and arrive at our victories. The more of us that do this, the stronger our profession becomes, which only serves to make all of our businesses more attractive to others in the future.

Until next time…

Enjoy the journey.

Wes Linden

P.S. Please feel free to visit my website for more generic tips, advice, videos and social media links:

www.weslinden.com

P.P.S. I do many free videos packed with top tips, advice, Q & A and interviews on my Facebook page - please 'like' the page to see more: www.facebook.com/WesLindenUK

About the Author

Wes was a student, already $10,000 in debt and living with his mother when he first heard about network marketing. Hoping to earn some money he decided to sign up and give it a go.

After a few months, Wes was hooked and eventually he dropped out of university.

Despite many of his friends and peers asking him, "*When are you going to get a proper job?*" and suggesting he had been tricked into a scam, Wes rode the storm and found himself financially semi- retired by the age of 24, and by 27 his residual income had overtaken the average salary of not just a teacher (the career for which he was destined), but a School Principal!

Wes has never had a "proper" job thanks to this profession and has only ever been involved with one networking business. He is still actively involved in his network marketing company as a distributor, having reached the top level, and has an annual team turnover in excess of $100m. In addition, he hosts many of his company's major conventions and presents some of their corporate recruiting and training videos.

In 2013, Wes became the first ever Brit to speak at the three-day Network Marketing Mastermind Event® in Orlando, alongside the biggest network marketing names in the world. In 2015 and 2016, he had been given the honor of being the host for the entire event. He is committed to the expansion of the profession and building its credibility worldwide. He believes this will be simpler when networkers from all companies link arms with each other.

Outside all of this, Wes is a keen traveller and has, on average, one vacation a month. He uses a personal trainer at least four times a week, in part to keep fit for his other major interest as a soccer referee, where Wes has officiated in the professional leagues up to Championship level for a number of years. He also enjoys spending lots of time with his close friends and family, and is a proud uncle to Noah.

It's thanks to the success he's achieved in network marketing that Wes has the choices to do these things whenever he wishes.

Can I book Wes to speak at my team or company event?

Plenty of others have, so why not ask the question?

Email speak@weslinden.com

What else has Wes done?

Well, a few things! But if you mean books and CDs, just the one so far – *79 Network Marketing Tips for Fast-Track Success*, as a book and 4-disc audio-book!

To order a copy go to www.weslinden.com/79tips

Can I bulk-buy Wes's books and CDs for my team?

Yes! There are bulk discounts for ten or more copies of this book as well as the *79 Network Marketing Tips* CD and book. Email bulk@weslinden.com

How can I connect with Wes?

Lots of ways! For free, generic training blogs, videos and interviews go to: www.weslinden.com

FACEBOOK FAN PAGE
www.facebook.com/WesLindenUK

TWITTER
@WesLinden

INSTAGRAM
@WesLinden

PERISCOPE
@WesLinden (or www.periscope.tv/weslinden)

YOUTUBE
www.youtube.com/weslinden

Be assured, Wes only provides generic training and so you and your team are safe to follow him!

Testimonials about Wes Linden

"Wes Linden is one of my favorites. His style is real and conversational and his stories are engaging and relevant. Thank you, Wes for your dedication, commitment and enthusiasm for the business of network marketing. You are a true gift."
Jordan Adler, Network Marketing Millionaire, Author of *Beach Money*

"Wes delivers powerful, practical ideas that will instantly boost your bottom line, as well as increase your belief for what is possible in the network marketing profession."
Sarah Robbins, Network Marketing Leader, Author of *Rock Your Network Marketing Business*

"I had the opportunity to finally hear Wes speak at The Network Marketing Mastermind Event® in Orlando, and he lived up to and blew past his impressive reputation. Few speakers today talk from actual heartfelt experience and authentic truth."
Richard Bliss Brooke, Author of *The Four Year Career* and *Mach II, The Art of Vision and Self Motivation*

"Words are just words unless you live by them. Wes Linden walks the talk!"
Hilde & Orjan Saele, Network Marketing Leaders, Author of *90 Days to Win*

"I first saw Wes speak at the prestigious Mastermind Event® and I became the latest in an ultra-long list of people whose respect and heart Wes had won. He got

the heart of our business right, because he had the right heart for it. And his sustained success is the clear result. Our profession, his company and team, the Mastermind community - we are all the richer because of this master relationship-builder and star-maker."
Donna Imson-Lecaroz, Network Marketing Leader and International Speaker

"When Wes speaks, I listen."
Margie Aliprandi, Network Marketing Leader, Author of *How to Get Absolutely Anything You Want*

"Some people catch you with their smile, then endear you with their thoughtful actions, kind spirit and humble heart. That's Wes Linden. He's built one of the most successful and sustainable organizations in Direct Selling by leading with a culture of friendship over business, principle over pride and caring over credentials. I consider Wes a peer, an inner circle mastermind, and above all a friends who never counts favors. When Wes shares from his journey, take notes…and apply them to your journey. You'll be glad you did."
Art Jonak, Mastermind Event® founder, entrepreneur and world-class networker

"By building a hugely successful business through a combination of hard work and genuinely supportive leadership, Wes has demonstrated that the good guys can win! Learn what it takes to get to the top and how to make friends on the journey!"
Andrew Lindsay MBE
CEO for a major Network Marketing Company, and Great Britain Olympic Gold Medalist

Acknowledgements

There will be thousands of people I've forgotten to mention here, who have played a part in my journey, so I apologize in advance.

But I will start by thanking some great mentors – Steve Critchley, for sage advice and helping me grow in my business; Robin Brooks, a great colleague and friend who is always fun to be around; plus Big Al for telling me I should be doing this and then telling me again and again! Art Jonak for his instant friendship and trust and for bringing the network marketing community together worldwide in the way I have tried (with many fine colleagues) to do in the UK. And Randy Gage for inspiring me when I first started in the profession and supporting my journey to become an ambassador in the profession.

To my Dad for giving me the sheer cheek to think I could do well in this profession. To my Mum for ensuring that I always believed I could succeed right from when I was in a crib. To Cheri and Justin for being wonderful and for giving us our lovely Noah.

To Steve, for the chats, the travels, the laughs and the unselfish support. To Tristan for his loyal friendship and ongoing encouragement. To Joga for being a great friend and excellent sounding board. To Jamie for more than 25 years of being a fantastic pal! To Malcolm – an incredible friend and ally. To Barry the Book for his enthusiasm and support on this project, especially when I really needed a push, as was my friend Mike!

To Patricia, Sian & Alison for the unwavering belief.

To the incredible trainers, speakers and leaders I have learned so much from.

To Justin, Wayne, Andrew and Charles who in so many ways made everything possible.

To Steve, Joe, Dan, Steph, Jimmy, Diana, Clive, Andy, Stav, Mark and Alex for their valuable lessons, help and feedback.

To all the incredible friends I have made in this profession, all over the world, mainly the distributors I meet from around the globe, irrespective of which company they represent. And of course, to the teammates I have the pleasure of working with and caring for.

What a fantastic profession – one that allows us to have fun, enjoy ourselves, help other people and make great money at the same time!

And thanks to my gone-but-not-forgotten great mates Ollie, JohnJo, Clive, Mairi and Bernell – who in lots of different ways, form part of my journey.

Made in the USA
Monee, IL
12 April 2021